SIMPLY BEAUTIFUL

A quiet unveiling of
the one thing no
mirror could fully
hold

MERCY NYAMANHINDI KWARAMBA

GULF BOOK
SERVICES

The contents of this work, including, but not limited to, the accuracy of events, people, and places depicted; opinions expressed; permission to use previously published materials included; and any advice given, or actions advocated are solely the responsibility of the author, who assumes all liabilities for the said work and indemnifies the publisher against any claims stemming from publication of the work.

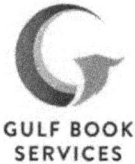

Published by Gulf Book Services Ltd
20 - 22 Wenlock Road, London,
NI 7GU, UK
Email: info@gulfbooks.co.uk
Office No: G23, Sharjah Publishing City Free Zone Sharjah – UAE

GULF BOOK SERVICES

First Published by Gulf Book Services Ltd

ISBN: 9781917529-26-6
Year: August 2025

DEDICATION

To my incredible boys, **Tadiwa** and **Anesu** this book is for you too.

Over the years, I have taught you to walk in truth, to stand tall in who you are, and to embrace your authenticity with quiet confidence. The world may try to define you by appearances, by labels, by the colour of your skin, I have heard it myself: "This one is lighter like the father; this one darker like the mother." But know this your value goes far beyond complexions and comments.

Your worth runs deeper than complexion. Who you are is far more powerful than how you look. My hope is that this book reminds you always to value what is within - character over image, substance over appearance.

May you always remember that real beauty starts from within. I hope and pray this book helps you build relationships rooted in character, not appearance and that you continue to see people and yourselves through the lens of truth, not trends.

Let this be your reminder:
The world does not define you.
You define how the world experiences your greatness.

With all my love,
Mom

ACKNOWLEDGMENTS

So many incredible people have touched my life, far too many to name. If I were to list each one, this book would be overflowing with names.

I have truly been blessed to meet and walk alongside amazing souls. To everyone who has supported me, encouraged me, challenged me, and inspired me along this journey: thank you. Your kindness and belief have meant more than words can say.

To my dear family, siblings, friends and my extended relatives your love and support have been my anchor.

A special thank you to my parents Bishop Cosmas and Angeline Nyamanhindi Chabarwa. It is your teachings and the values you instilled in me as I grew that have shaped who I am today.

Above all, I thank God for giving me the strength, the wisdom, and the grace to bring this vision to life.

PREFACE

Before you journey through these pages, let me share something from my heart.

This book is not a rebellion against the values, beliefs, or faith that ground us. It does not stand in opposition to the timeless wisdom we hold dear, the teachings that shape our lives, our morals, and our character. In fact, I believe with all my soul that our spiritual foundations and personal authenticity can and should co-exist beautifully.

When I speak of becoming yourself, of stepping fully into who you are, it is not an invitation to disregard the guidance of your faith or disrespect the principles that give your life meaning. This book does not dismiss the teachings that call us to humility, kindness, integrity, or reverence. It simply asks that, within those teachings, you find the freedom to honor your individuality and to embrace the person you were uniquely created to be.

We live in a world that often demands conformity in places it was never meant to. It tries to squeeze us into molds that have nothing to do with our character or calling, but everything to do with fleeting trends, shallow expectations, or someone else's comfort. In that process, too many of us dim our light, hide our laughter, doubt our worth, and lose sight of the masterpiece we walk in faith and still be fully, vibrantly yourself. That being "you" does not mean discarding the truths that matter most, it means bringing your true self under their guidance, not someone else's version of who you should be.

So as you turn these pages, know this: your faith, your convictions, your moral compass they are safe here. This book will not ask you to abandon them. Instead, I hope it will help you live them out with an authenticity that is undeniably yours.

Because there is power in knowing who you are. And even greater power in being that person, beautifully and unapologetically, all while honoring the One who made you - God and the values that sustain you.

Welcome. I am so glad you are here.

CONTENTS

INTRODUCTION

"True beauty is about standing tall in your authenticity and celebrating who you were always meant to be."

Imagine waking up tomorrow and seeing yourself not as society tells you to, but as you truly are; flawless, whole, and more than enough. For so long, we have been told that to be beautiful, we must change. We must fit into someone else's mold, follow a prescribed standard, and strive to meet unrealistic expectations. We scroll through social media, where beauty is filtered, enhanced, and curated to perfection. We walk through life surrounded by messages telling us that we are not enough, unless we look a certain way.

But what if everything we have been taught about beauty is wrong? What if you were always beautiful, just as you are? What if you didn't need to change anything about yourself to be loved, seen, or valued? This book is about embracing the truth that the most authentic beauty lies within you. It is about realizing that you were never meant to look like anyone else. You were meant to be exactly who you are, perfect in your imperfections, beautiful in your authenticity, and whole without any need for validation from the outside world.

In these pages, I want to take you on a journey, a journey of rediscovery. A journey to embrace the beauty that already exists within you, waiting to be acknowledged. Together, we will break free from the constraints of societal standards and learn to celebrate the unique qualities that make you, *you*. Your true beauty is not defined by your appearance; it is defined by your essence, by your heart, your soul, and your unwavering authenticity.

This book is not just about how you look; it is about how you feel. It is about accepting yourself fully and loving yourself completely. It is about letting go of the idea that you need to fit into someone else's idea of beauty and instead defining beauty on your own terms.

I know that for many of us, the journey to self-acceptance is not an easy one. We have spent years doubting ourselves, comparing ourselves, and trying to be something we are not. But this is your moment to stop pretending and to start living your truth. The moment to embrace your natural, unfiltered beauty.

You are worthy. You are enough. You are beautiful, just as you are, and when you realize that everything changes. The way you see yourself, the way you interact with the world, and the way the world sees you. Because beauty that comes from authenticity is magnetic, it is the kind of beauty that does not need validation because it is rooted in something real, something undeniable.

This book is written because someone, somewhere, needs to hear this:
You do not need lighter skin to be radiant.
You do not need smaller features to be seen.
You do not need society's permission to know you are beautiful. Let us begin this journey of embracing your true beauty inside and out. Because you are simply beautiful

1. FLAWLESS IMPERFECTIONS

"True beauty is not in perfection but in the courage to embrace your imperfections with pride."

W hat if the very flaws you wish to hide are the unique strokes that make your portrait extraordinary? We have all stood in front of the mirror, searching for things we could change. A smoother complexion, a slimmer waist, the perfect hair, the perfect body. But what if I told you that these *"imperfections"* you so desperately wish to erase are actually the very things that make you unique, beautiful, and irreplaceable?

It is easy to believe that beauty means perfection. Society, with its filters and airbrushed images, has convinced us that if we do not look a certain way, we are somehow not enough. But here is the truth: The quest for perfection is an illusion, and the beauty we seek is right in front of us, in the very things we often wish to hide.

Our imperfections are not mistakes; they are marks of our humanity. They are the traces of our life's story, the evidence of our experiences, and the things that make us, *us*. Imagine, for a moment, a world where no one cared about fitting into a mold, where everyone simply embraced who they are, flaws and all. It would be a world full of unique, powerful individuals, each radiating their own brand of beauty.

What if instead of hiding our imperfections, we began to celebrate them? What if we recognized that our scars, our stretch marks, our skin color, and our "flaws" are the true reflections of our strength and authenticity? When we choose to embrace our imperfections, we unlock a kind of beauty that cannot be replicated or stolen. This beauty is yours alone, a masterpiece shaped by every experience, every struggle, every triumph.

It is time to redefine what beauty truly is. It is not about conforming to a set of standards that were never meant for you. It is about accepting, loving, and honoring who you are right now, as you are. Because the world does not need another cookie-cutter image of beauty, it needs the real you, in all your authentic and imperfects.

True beauty does not ask for permission to exist. It is simply there, waiting to be acknowledged. And when you finally give yourself permission to see the beauty in your imperfections, you will start to see it everywhere in yourself, in others, and in the world around you.

So, the next time you look in the mirror, do not focus on what you wish was different. Instead, focus on what makes you uniquely you. Because *you* are beautiful, just as you are.

2. THE INSPIRATION BEHIND THE WORDS

"True beauty begins the moment you stop comparing yourself to others and start embracing your own unique radiance."

C an a single word, a passing comment, or a seemingly harmless joke shape the way you see yourself for years to come? As I sit here, reflecting on the journey that led me to write this book, I cannot help but think about the early years of my childhood. Growing up, I often felt the weight of society's narrow definition of beauty. In the community I was raised in, being light-skinned was seen as the standard of beauty. I remember hearing comments that irritated me a bit, casual words that linked beauty to being light-skinned and ugliness to being dark-skinned. Phrases like *"That beautiful light-skinned girl"* or *"That ugly dark girl"* were tossed around without thought, but their impact ran deep to many. They did not just describe appearances; they planted beliefs, quietly telling us who was worthy of admiration and who was not. These words, though spoken casually made a lasting impression on me.

One moment that stands out in my memory is when a relative made a joke about me and my brother. He was light-skinned, and she said, "Your brother is Fanta, and you are Coke." To her, it was a harmless joke, but to me, as a young child, it made me feel different. It planted a seed of doubt in my mind, making me question whether I was truly beautiful. I could not help but compare myself to my brother and others around me, believing that if I were just lighter, I would be seen as beautiful too.

Years ago, when one of my close friends was about to get married, a relative asked the husband a question that really surprised me *"Is she light-skinned or dark-skinned?"*. When he answered, *"She is dark,"* the relative paused, almost disappointed, and said, *"Oh, why?"*. It was not until they met my friend in person that they changed their opinion saying, *"Well, she is not bad."* Imagine that someone questioning your value without ever even knowing you based on nothing but your skin tone.

Not long after I got married, I attended a function where I ran into an older woman, a close family friend. She smiled warmly, and then without hesitation asked a question that caught me completely off guard. "Where did you find a light-skinned guy?" I stood there, stunned for a moment. I smiled politely, but inside, something shifted. It was not the question itself that hurt, it was what it revealed. A quiet, unquestioned belief shaped by society, that being with someone light-skinned somehow made me more validated, more beautiful, more "worthy." In that moment, I realized just how deeply rooted these ideas are. How the world, without even knowing it, teaches us that light is better, more desirable, more worthy. And how those beliefs try to define not just what we should admire but who we believe we are.

Years ago, I remember when skin bleaching products started showing up in stores across my country. The advertisements promised lighter skin, a new look, a better life. I remember some friends encouraging me to try them - to change my complexion, to "enhance" what I was born with. But something in me resisted. I thought to myself, how strange it would be to suddenly wake up with lighter skin, when everyone had known me my whole life as the dark-skinned girl. It felt dishonest, like I would be hiding the very thing that told the story of who I was. So I chose to stay true to myself. I chose to embrace my birth color.

Sadly, I know many who did try those products. Some of them suffered terrible side effects, and their skin changed permanently. What was once a pursuit of beauty became a source of pain. It broke my heart to see how far we were willing to go just to be accepted by someone else's standard.

It would be easy to brush off moments like these. It is easy to pretend they do not matter, but the truth is they do. They leave lasting impressions. They silently build cages around your self-esteem. They make you question if you are truly enough, exactly as you are.

But here is the thing, those experiences did not define me. They did not define my worth and they certainly did not define my beauty. I am so incredibly grateful for the foundation my parents gave me. They did not raise me to place value on external beauty but to be confident, to respect myself, and to love who I was. Beauty was never a topic they emphasized in our home. Instead, they taught us to stand tall, to be proud of who we were, and to never allow anyone or anything to define our worth by how we looked. Confidence was not something they taught through words, it was something they instilled through their actions, through the way they carried themselves and the way they encouraged us to embrace our uniqueness.

Their love and support gave me the strength to see beyond the narrow beauty standards of my community. I eventually realized that my dark skin, my uniqueness, was a part of what made me beautiful. It was not about conforming to the world's idea of beauty, it was about embracing who I truly was.

This book is the result of that journey which is about standing firm in our authenticity and celebrating the beauty that lies within every one of us. I want to share this with you because I know I am not alone in feeling that society has made us question our worth based on how we look. I want to remind you that no matter what the world tells you, your beauty is not defined by your skin tone, your shape, or any other external factor. Your beauty is in your authenticity, your heart, and your confidence.

I wrote this book to show you that you are more than enough, just as you are.
Your beauty is not shade, a shape, or a size.
Your beauty is your story.
Your beauty is your confidence.
Your beauty is you: unapologetically, beautifully, and wonderfully you.

You are Simply Beautiful.
And no one—*no comment, no joke, no standard*—can take that away from you.

3. BEYOND THE MIRROR

"Your value cannot be measured by the frame of a reflection, it resides in the brilliance of your authenticity."

Have you ever looked in the mirror and wondered why it feels like your reflection is judging you more than anyone else? We stand in front of mirrors more often than we realize checking for flaws, adjusting clothes, analyzing our bodies, hoping the reflection will say, "You are beautiful." But instead, too often, we hear, *"Not yet! Not quite! Not enough!"*

Let us get real for a second, that mirror! It does not hold the power to define your worth. It only shows what is on the outside. What it does not show is your strength, your kindness, and your soul. And that is the part that makes you truly beautiful.

You know those moments; you catch your reflection and immediately start criticizing. *"Why does my nose look like that? Why can't my stomach be flatter? Why can't I just look like her?"* But guess what? That voice in your head, it is not the truth. It is just a loud echo of what the world has tried to teach you about beauty and it is wrong.

We have been conditioned to use mirrors like measurement tools judging every wrinkle, every stretch mark, every imperfection. But you were not put on this earth to be measured. You were born to be seen not just by others, but most importantly, by yourself.

11

The mirror reflects your image, but it will never capture the depth of your soul's beauty. The mirror has a way of holding up more than just your reflection. It shows you the physical features that you have become so familiar with, the curve of your smile, the shape of your eyes, the shade of your skin. But often, it also reflects something deeper: the stories you have been told about yourself, the comparisons you have made, and the standards you have felt pressured to meet.

As a teenager, I could not look in the mirror without hearing the echo of society's voice in my head. *"If only your skin were lighter"*. *"If only your features were different."* The mirror was not just showing me; it was showing me all the ways I thought I was not enough. I thought I was looking at flaws, but what I was really seeing were the scars left by comparison and unrealistic expectations.

But here is the truth the mirror won't tell you, it cannot see the most beautiful parts of you. It cannot see your resilience, your kindness, or the way your laughter lights up a room. It does not reflect your courage or your dreams. The mirror only reflects the surface, and yet we allow it to dictate so much of how we see ourselves.

The real tragedy is not that we believe what the mirror shows us it is that we forget everything it does not. To truly see yourself, you must go beyond the mirror. You must look inward. Beauty is not just skin deep; it is found in the way you show up for others, in the way you chase your dreams, and in the way you own your story. It is in your essence, your spirit, and your authenticity. And those things can never be captured by glass and silver.

When I started seeing myself beyond the reflection, everything changed. I stopped looking for flaws and started looking for truth. I realized that my worth was not tied to the size of my waist, my hip size or the shade of my skin. It was not tied to my reflection at all. It was tied to how I chose to live, love, and embrace the person I was created to be.

If you have ever felt trapped by what you see in the mirror, I want to tell you something: you are so much more than what you see. Your beauty is not a measurement; it is a presence. It is not something you need validation for it is something you own, something you wear with pride because it is yours alone.

The next time you stand in front of the mirror, ask yourself: am I looking at the real me, or am I letting the world define what I see? Then, remind yourself of this truth: the mirror is only a tool it cannot define your value, and it will never capture your full, radiant beauty. That is something only you can own.

The next time you stand in front of a mirror, remember it reflects a body but it can never define a soul.

4. THE POWER OF BEING YOU

"You are enough, just as you are a masterpiece of individuality in a world hungry for replicas.

In a world that thrives on conformity, standing firm as your true self is a progressive act. There is a magic in being unapologetically yourself, a kind of power that no one else can replicate. But in a world that constantly pushes us to conform to trends, expectations, and ideals, it is easy to lose sight of this truth. Being yourself does not just make you unique; it makes you unstoppable.

Yet, being yourself often feels like the hardest thing to do. Society encourages blending in, but the irony is that the people we admire the most are those who stand out. Think about it: the trailblazers, the innovators, the icons they did not succeed because they followed the crowd. They succeeded because they leaned into who they were, flaws and all.

But what does it really mean to "be yourself"? And why does it feel so intimidating at times? You were never meant to be a copy. You were designed to be original. And yes, that takes courage, real courage, because being different means standing alone sometimes. It means being misunderstood. It means showing up in a world that often expects you to tone it down, when your spirit was built to shine.

Here is the truth, everything extraordinary about you, the parts you have been told are too loud, too bold, too much that is where your beauty lives. Have you ever found yourself shrinking in a room full of people just to be accepted? Changing your tone, your look, your laughter, your walk? We have all been there. We have all felt the pressure to conform, especially when it feels like everyone else fits a mold you were never made to fit.

For me, this journey has been a series of small awakenings. I have always been strong-willed, not a pushover. I am the kind of person who seeks to understand things deeply, who questions what does not make sense, who speaks up when something does not sit right. If I am not sure, I will ask. If I am unhappy, I will say it. It is who I am.

But here is what I have learned: not everyone knows how to handle that. Over the years, I have encountered people who seemed almost intimidated by this part of me. Instead of engaging, they would try to dim it, make me feel like asking questions was being difficult, or speaking up was being confrontational. For a while, it worked. I doubted myself, wondering if perhaps I should just nod along, stay silent, and blend in also if l was really a bad person by doing so.

However, time and age have a way of revealing truths. I started to notice there were just as many people if not more who actually valued this trait. Who admired my willingness to question, to stand firm, to seek clarity. They were drawn to honest conversations and realness, to relationships where nothing had to be hidden or tiptoed around. That is the thing about being you: it might repel some, but it will deeply resonate with others. The right people will like or love you not despite your strong will, your curiosity, or your voice but because of it. So, keep being bold enough to speak up and strong enough to stand when needed because there is power in being exactly who you are.

Let me remind you fitting in is not the goal. *Belonging while being yourself is.* There is a difference between the two, belonging asks you to come exactly as you are. The courage to be different is not just about appearance. It is about embracing your natural beauty when the world tries to convince you that you need fixing. It is about speaking up when staying silent would be safer. It is about choosing to live by your values when it is easier to follow the crowd.

I once heard a mentor say something that left a lasting impression on me. He said, *"I do not compromise my values just to make people happy. There are certain things I simply won't do. And if people cannot understand that it is okay. I will always stand by my values."* There was something so freeing in those words. He was not angry, he was not defensive, he was simply grounded, rooted and unshaken by whether or not others approved of his decision, **that is courage, that is power.**

There is power in being the one who does not conform. The one who wears her hair the way it grows, who shows her skin the way it shines, who carries her body the way it was built. You show others that it is okay to embrace themselves too. You give them permission to stop hiding.

Your difference is not your weakness it is your gift, and do not let anyone tell you that being different means being less than. Look around at the people who have changed the world, who have left a mark they were not the ones who followed. They were the ones who dared to be different. Who dared to say, *this is me, and I am not afraid of being seen.*

Being authentic is about honesty. It is about honouring the truth of who you are, even when it is uncomfortable. Some people may never understand it, that is okay. You are not for everyone and you do not need to be.

I think of my father when I say this. A man of great integrity, his yes was always a yes, his no always a firm no. In his work, he came across people who tried to take advantage of the system who were comfortable bending rules and compromising standards. But my father never wavered, he did not bend to be popular and he did not compromise to win approval. And yes, to some people, he became a stumbling block. They did not like his conviction; they did not like his honesty. They did not like that they could not manipulate him. But for the ones who valued truth? Who wanted to do things the right way? He was the kind of person they trusted. The kind they wanted by their side. What struck me most was this: even when he knew some people did not like him for standing his ground, he did not change. He did not soften his standards just to be accepted. He understood something powerful *being respected is far greater than being liked*. That is what it means to be authentic: but deeply rooted, not rebellious but real.

What matters most is that *you* understand your worth, that you honour your beauty, that you walk with your head high, not because the world tells you that you are beautiful but because you finally believe it yourself.

Here is something magical: when you have the courage to be different, you attract the people who are meant for you. The ones who love you for who you are, not for who you pretend to be. The ones who see your uniqueness and say, *thank you for not hiding*. Stop waiting for someone to validate the beauty of your uniqueness.

Your laugh? Beautiful.

Your boldness? Needed.

Your scars? Proof you survived.

Your background? A gift, not a burden.

You are not too much.

You are not too little.

You are powerfully, purposefully, beautifully enough, just as you are.

SIMPLY BEAUTIFUL

5. THE FEAR OF JUDGEMENT

"The boldest act of self-love is showing up as yourself in a world that taught you to hide."

The biggest barrier to being yourself is the fear of what others might think. *"What if they do not like me?"* *"What if they think I'm too much or not enough?"* These questions echo in our minds more often than we admit. We carry them into conversations, decisions, even the clothes we wear or the photos we choose to post online. It is a silent pressure that sneaks into the background of our lives, convincing us to shrink, to soften, to stay quiet, and to play small.

But here is the truth: people will always have opinions. No matter how perfect you try to be, someone will still misunderstand you, criticize you, or judge you. You could mold yourself into a dozen different versions, and still, not everyone will approve. So why not be you? Why not take all that energy spent trying to fit in and use it to stand out as your true self?

Fear of judgement is like an invisible fence. You may not see it, but it stops you from running free. It whispers, do not wear that, they will laugh. Do not speak up, they will think you are arrogant. Do not try that, you will fail, and so you hold back. You let dreams slide, you bite your tongue, you settle.

I have met people who wear masks every day, afraid to let their light shine because someone once told them it was "too bright." I have seen brilliant women dull their sparkle, creatives abandon their calling all because they feared being judged. But here is what I have also learned: when someone chooses to live authentically, despite the fear, something shifts. There is power in showing up as you are. That power is contagious.

It takes courage to be seen. It takes strength to stand in your truth when the world is more comfortable with you pretending. But every time you choose truth over fear, you get a little stronger. Every time you say, *"This is who I am"* the fear loses its grip.

Judgement will come, yes but so will admiration, respect, and deep, genuine connection. Because people are drawn to what is real, the right people will celebrate your authenticity. The rest? They were never your people to begin with.

Letting go of the fear of judgement does not mean you stop caring about others. It simply means you stop letting their opinions define your worth. You begin to understand that your voice matters, your choices matter, and your truth deserves space.

So speak up, even if your voice trembles. Wear those colourful clothes that makes you feel alive. Pursue the dream that excites you, even if it scares others. Say no when something does not align with your values. There is nothing more beautiful than someone who is unapologetically themselves.

The fear of judgement may always whisper, but your courage gets the final word. And in that courage, you will discover the kind of confidence that no approval can give and no opinion can take away.

6. OWNING YOUR STORY

"Your story is not a flaw; it is your fingerprint, own it."

Your story every twist, every turn, every triumph, and every setback are what makes you uniquely you. No one else on this planet has lived your life. No one else has your exact perspective, your talents, or your dreams. That is your superpower.

People do not connect with perfection; they connect with authenticity. So, own your quirks, own your voice, own the parts of yourself that you have been told to hide. They are what make you, *you*.

I was born and raised in Zimbabwe, in a vibrant, loud, and beautiful high-density suburb. Resources were limited, but joy was abundant. We did not have it all, but we had enough to laugh, to play, and to build dreams. We ran barefoot in the sun, played outside the house until dark, and made the best out of what we had. It was a childhood full of love, energy, and endless stories.

That childhood shaped me in ways I am still discovering. Growing up, I developed a loud voice and an even louder laugh both of which were nurtured in a family full of people with great sense of humour. We cracked jokes over simple meals, laughed about everything, and found joy even in the ordinary. Humour was our therapy, and our love language.

23

Now fast forward to the corporate world, a world filled with polished presentations, poised conversations, and polite laughter. I have tried, *trust me,* I have tried to lower my voice, to soften my tone, to present myself in a way that fits the image of "corporate voice." But somehow, no matter how much I try, the unfiltered, real me finds its way out. My laugh bursts out before I can suppress it, my voice rises with passion, and suddenly I am that little girl again, unfiltered and full of life.

I have come to realize that there is no reason to hide her. Why should I bury the parts of me that are most alive, most real, most rooted in truth? I was not raised to pretend. I was raised to show up, to be present, to be seen and I cannot be like someone who grew up differently. We do not all come from the same mold, and that is the beauty of it.

So many of us have been taught to edit ourselves to trim our stories, to hide our roots, to be more "digestible" for the sake of acceptance. But here is the truth: shrinking yourself never makes room for growth. What makes you different is what makes you powerful.

Owning my story is also what led me to write a book about dealing with the loss of a baby *Mothers of Angels.* In it, I shared a deeply personal experience of grief and healing, one that many would have kept hidden, tucked behind polite smiles and unspoken pain. For some, speaking openly about such loss was seen as taboo something to be whispered about, if at all. To others, it seemed like a display of weakness in a world obsessed with strength and perfection. But I chose to speak. I chose to write. Not because I wanted pity, but because I understood that unspoken pain becomes an invisible prison.

We live in a time where everyone is trying to look like they have it all together; no wounds, no failures, no heartbreaks. And yet behind those perfectly curated lives are stories yearning to be acknowledged. Pretending to be okay when you are not, does not make you strong. It makes you silent. And silence, over time, breaks the soul. When I chose to own my truth and share it with the world, something powerful happened, other women began to open up to me. They told me their stories, their losses, their hidden pain.

What I learned is this: vulnerability does not weaken us. It connects us. Our stories, especially the ones soaked in sorrow are sacred. They are the fingerprints of who we are becoming. So tell yours. Not for validation, but for liberation. Because what once broke you may just be the very thing that sets someone else free.

Your story matters. Your laughter, your accent, your background, your scars all matter. They tell the world where you come from, how far you have come, and where you are going. When you hide them, you rob the world of your magic.

So, speak with your full voice.
Laugh with your whole heart.
Walk with the rhythm of your own story.
Be proud of the road you have walked even if it was not paved or perfect. The dust on your feet is part of your beauty. You are not a copy of someone else's journey. You are an original, a masterpiece in progress. And the more you own your story, the more you give others permission to own theirs.

Your story does not have to be polished to be powerful. It only needs to be true. Own every part of it, because it is yours and no one else can live it like you do.

SIMPLY BEAUTIFUL

7. BEYOND SKIN DEEP

"Real beauty begins where the eyes cannot see."

What people see on the outside is just the surface, your beauty goes much deeper. Beauty that cannot be seen is the kind that touches hearts and leaves an eternal impression. True beauty reveals itself not in the seen, but is felt - in laughter, kindness, and resilience.

"What if the most beautiful thing about you is not what the mirror reflects, but what your presence makes others feel?" We live in a world obsessed with appearances, flawless skin, perfect hair, the right body type. Society places so much value on the visible that we forget about the beauty that cannot be seen, but here is the truth: beauty is more than skin deep. The most powerful, lasting kind of beauty is the kind you cannot touch, but you can feel.

Think about it, have you ever met someone who radiates warmth? Someone whose presence makes you feel seen, valued, and understood? You may not remember what they were wearing or whether their features fit society's definition of "perfect," but you remember how they made you feel.

We have been conditioned to think of beauty as something external, something that can be captured in a photograph or measured by the number of likes on a social media post. But have you ever stopped to ask yourself: Who decided what is beautiful? And why should their definition be the one we live by?

Beauty, real beauty, begins beneath the surface. It is in the way you carry pain with grace. It is in the kindness you offer when no one is watching. It is in your voice when you speak truth, and in your silence when you choose peace over pride.

Let me say this loud and clear:
- ❖ You are not your skin
- ❖ You are not your size
- ❖ You are not your flaws or your features.

You are the fire inside, the soul that breathes, the heart that beats and that is what makes you radiant.

The world may praise flawless skin, sculpted bodies, and symmetrical faces but none of that guarantees goodness, joy, or depth. External beauty fades, trends change but the way you love, the way you lift others, the light you bring into the room? That leaves a mark.

Have you ever met someone who was not conventionally attractive but had a presence that pulled you in? That spark in their laugh, that confidence in their stride, that warmth in their spirit you could not stop looking. That is beyond skin deep, that is the beauty we remember and that is the beauty that matters.

And yes, it is okay to want to look good. To style your hair, to wear your favourite lipstick, to feel good in your clothes, *I also do the same* but the foundation of your beauty cannot be built on things that fade, because the day you wake up with no makeup, messy hair, and puffy eyes you are still beautiful. Because you are still *you*.

Your beauty is in your story, in the way you have risen from hurt. In the way you keep going when it would be easier to quit. In the way you smile when you could cry. In the way you love even when your heart is still healing. That is beauty and no mirror, no filter, no scale can measure that.

You do not have to compete with the world's definition of beauty. You do not have to compare yourself to what you see online. You are already equipped with something most people are still searching for *depth*, and that kind of beauty cannot be faked. Stop shrinking your worth to fit into someone else's mold. Stop dimming your light to make others comfortable, stop believing that your appearance is your most valuable trait.

Instead, nurture your soul, develop your character, walk with compassion, pour confidence into yourself like it is a daily procedure because it should be. When you invest in the person within, everything on the outside shines brighter. That is when your presence becomes unforgettable.

People may forget what you wore. They may forget the exact shape of your face or the way your hair looked, but they will never forget how you made them feel. They will never forget your energy, your kindness, your authenticity. That is the beauty that outlives the moment.

So do not just be beautiful, be *simply* beautiful. A beauty that glows in the dark, a beauty that does not need approval to exist. You already have it in you.

True beauty does not demand attention, it commands respect because the most powerful kind of beauty is not skin-deep, it is soul deep.

8. BREAKING FREE FROM COMPARISONS

"Your worth is not measured by someone else's reflection. You were never meant to compete you were born to shine in your own light."

The moment you stop comparing is the moment you start living. One of the most liberating truths you will ever learn is this: **You are not in competition with anyone.** Your journey is your own, your timing is divine, your story is unfolding exactly as it should. Comparison creeps in quietly, it shows up on social media when someone seems to be doing better. It whispers in family gatherings when someone else gets praised for something you have worked hard for. It even disguises itself as motivation but instead of lifting you, it weighs you down.

Comparison is the thief of joy, the destroyer of identity, and the fast lane to insecurity. We have all been there looking at someone else's life and wondering, *'why do I not have her skin? Why is her career moving faster? Why does her life seem more perfect?'* But here is the truth you need to hear it repeatedly: **You are not them and that is your power.**

Comparing yourself to others is like comparing the sun to the moon. They both shine, but at different times and in different ways. One does not have to dim for the other to glow. The sky is big enough for both to be brilliant and so is this world.

When you stop measuring your worth against someone else's highlight reel, you start to see the beauty in your own path. You start to notice the quiet victories, the strength it took to get out of bed today. The grace you extended when no one was watching. The battles you have overcome that no one even knows about.

You start to realize that your uniqueness is not something to be hidden. It is something to be celebrated. You see, no one else has your voice, no one else carries your exact perspective, your rhythm, your fire. And that means the world needs *you* to show up, not as a copy of someone else but as the most *authentic* version of you.

There is no greater power than the power of being yourself. It is a power that cannot be replicated, stolen, or diminished. Step into it, own it. Let the world see you for who you are unapologetically and wholeheartedly. Know this: when you embrace the power of being you, you do not just change your own life, you light the way for others to do the same. You give them permission to stop comparing and start becoming.

You are already more than enough. So, wear the color that makes you feel alive. Speak the language of your heart. Walk like you belong because you do. There is courage in authenticity, and in that courage, you will find freedom. *Comparison ends where confidence begins. The more you embrace who you are, the less you will need to look sideways because everything you need is already within you.*

9. REDEFINING BEAUTY STANDARDS

"Shatter the mold. Let your own reflection surprise you."

Who decided what beauty should look like and why did we ever let them decide for us? Let us be honest: most of the beauty standards we have grown up with were not made with all of us in mind. They were shaped by media, culture, and generations of messages that told us we had to look a certain way to be worthy: worthy of love, attention, success and even happiness.

If you did not meet those standards? You were expected to change yourself until you did. Lighter skin, straight hair, small-pointed nose, thinner waist, curves in all the "right" places and the list goes on. For years, we have watched as these narrow ideals were sold to us on TV screens, in magazines, on billboards, and now, in the palm of our hands through social media.

But here is the truth: those standards were never universal. They were never fair and they were never rooted in what truly matters. They were created to make people feel *"not enough."* Because when you feel like you are not enough, you start buying products, procedures and promises. The entire industry is built on making us chase something that was never real in the first place.

It is time to change that.

It is time to redefine what beauty means on our terms.
Because beauty does not belong to one race, one body type, one
hairstyle, or one skin tone.

It is everywhere.
It is in the gap between someone's teeth when they smile.
It is in textured hair that defies gravity.
It is in a body that has carried life, carried pain, carried
resilience.
It is in the quiet confidence of someone who finally knows their
worth.

Redefining beauty does not mean we throw out everything that
is celebrated it means we make room for more. We open the
doors wide enough for everyone to walk through without
needing to shrink themselves and that includes you.

You do not need to meet someone else's standard to be beautiful.
You set your own standard. You are your own definition. And
when you stand in that truth boldly, confidently, unapologetically
you give others permission to do the same.

This shift starts in small, everyday moments. Like looking in the
mirror and choosing to affirm what you love about yourself
instead of what you want to change. Like complimenting
someone on their energy instead of just their outfit. Like showing
up in your natural beauty and not apologizing for it.

It is in how we raise our sons and daughters and how we speak
to ourselves. It is in what we share online and how we show up
in real life. It is in rejecting toxic comparisons and embracing
individuality like the sacred thing it is.

You are not too dark.

You are not too light.

You are not too curvy, too thin, too tall, too short.

You are *just right* exactly as you are.

When we stop trying to meet standards and start becoming our own, we stop performing and start living. We free ourselves; we breathe easier, we grow differently and that glow? It is contagious, it changes rooms, it shifts conversations and it creates a new normal.

Redefining beauty starts with understanding that the standards we have been taught are not only limiting they are exclusionary. They tell a single story of beauty when the reality is that beauty is as diverse as humanity itself.

Look around you. True beauty exists in every shade, every shape, every size. It is in the woman with laugh lines etched into her face from years of joy. It is in the man with deep scars that tell stories of resilience. It is in the teenager who wears their natural hair with pride, despite years of being told it was "unprofessional" or "unmanageable."

Everywhere you turn, beauty exists not because it fits a mold, but because it is real, it is authentic, and it is unapologetically unique.

10. YOUR ROLE IN REDEFINING BEAUTY

"You are not just part of the beauty conversation; you are the definition."

Here is the thing: redefining beauty is not just a global drive, it is a personal one. It does not begin with billboards or magazines. It starts in our mirrors, in our conversations, in the quiet moments where we decide to see ourselves differently. It is not just about changing how we see others. It is about transforming how we see ourselves.

We have been taught loudly that we need to fit in to be beautiful. That we must meet some ever-shifting standard to be worthy. But what if we unlearned that? What if we stopped measuring beauty by someone else's ruler and embraced the truth: that we are beautiful simply because we are?

Every time you choose to love yourself exactly as you are, you are shaking the system. Every time you look in the mirror and choose affirmation over criticism, you are pushing back against decades of conditioning. Every time you compliment someone on their strength, their kindness, or their energy instead of just their appearance, you are rewriting the rules. And it matters, it all matters. Because you do not need a massive platform to make a difference. You just need to show up as your whole, honest self and give others permission to do the same.

I remember once meeting a young girl who kept straightening her natural hair because she thought her curls were not "presentable" enough. One day, she saw me wearing my own hair in its natural state, full and unpressed. She stared for a long moment and then smiled shyly. "I did not know we could wear it like that," she said. That one moment was not about hair it was about possibility, visibility and permission.

This is what redefining beauty looks like in real time.

It is not always loud. Sometimes it is a whisper, a decision, a shared truth. So, what if we created a new definition of beauty? What if beauty was not about being admired but about being authentic?

Here is mine:

- **Beauty is confidence**: the way you carry yourself when you know your worth.
- **Beauty is authenticity**: showing up as your true self, unfiltered and unapologetic.
- **Beauty is kindness**: the light you bring to the world through your actions and your heart.

When beauty is defined like this, it stops being something you chase and starts being something you live. It becomes accessible, inclusive and limitless. Redefining beauty is a collective effort, but it starts with you. In the choices you make, in the words you speak, in the love you give yourself and reflect to others. You have a role in this revolution. Not because you need to prove anything, but because simply by being yourself, you already are.

11. THE LIBERATION OF SELF-ACCEPTANCE

In self-acceptance, the real story begins.

Self-acceptance is not surrender, it is self-celebration. What if the only thing standing between you and true freedom is your own reflection? For years, we are conditioned to chase an ideal, an impossible standard of beauty, success, and worthiness that is always just out of reach. We learn to measure ourselves against others, seeking validation in compliments, achievements, or the approval of people who do not even know our hearts. And in that endless pursuit, we forget the most important thing: *We were already enough before we ever tried to prove it.*

We all want to be liked. It is human nature, but when your sense of worth depends on the opinions of others, you become a prisoner of their expectations. Think about it. How many times have you held back your thoughts for fear of being judged? How often have you changed parts of yourself your style, your voice, your dreams just to fit in?

Now ask yourself this: *What if I stopped trying to fit in and started standing out as my true self?* The most powerful shift happens when you realize that no one else's opinion should have the power to define you. The day you stop seeking validation is the day you set yourself free.

Self-acceptance is not the end of the journey, it is the foundation for a life lived fully and freely. It is not about "settling" or refusing to grow. It is about finally dropping the weight of expectations and choosing to embrace yourself, as you are, in this moment. Because here's the truth: *you will never be free until you stop waiting for permission to be yourself.*

We have been taught to hustle for our worth. To constantly improve, fix, and perfect ourselves until we feel "ready." Ready to be seen., ready to be loved, ready to be enough. But here's the truth we are not told: **you do not need to earn self-acceptance.** You just need to *allow* it.

Self-acceptance does not mean you give up on growth. It means you love yourself in every stage of the journey. It means you stop waiting until you lose the weight, clear the skin, or change your hair to finally say, "I like me." That moment, that's liberation. Because when you stop fighting yourself, you reclaim all the energy you have been pouring into self-judgment. You stop living to impress and start living in peace. You become free.

And wow, what a beautiful kind of freedom that is. Let us be honest. Self-acceptance is radical in a world that profits from your self-doubt. It is a rebellion, a quiet revolution. When you accept yourself your quirks, your scars, your story you tell the world, *"You do not get to decide my worth. I do."*

There's nothing more magnetic than someone who walks into a room not trying to prove anything. Someone who just *is.* At ease with who they are. Unapologetic. Grounded. You do not get there by pretending. You get there by doing the work the inner work. The brave work. The soul-deep work of unlearning shame, releasing comparison, and replacing self-criticism with self-kindness.

You have every right to love yourself as you are right now. Not the future you. Not the "fixed" version. Not the one who has it all together. Just *you*. The one breathing in this moment. That is enough. Stop waiting to feel beautiful when you have "arrived." You have already arrived.

You can still strive, grow and evolve. But do it from a place of love, not lack. Accepting yourself does not mean you think you are perfect. It means you believe you are worthy even with your imperfections.

And that worth? It is not up for debate. Let us flip the narrative. Let us stop saying, "I will love myself when..." and start saying, "I choose to love myself now."

The truth is no one sees your "flaws" the way you do. Most people do not notice that little thing you obsess over in the mirror. And the ones who matter? They see your heart, your energy, your spirit. And once *you* start seeing those things in yourself too, everything changes.

You stop needing to be chosen, you choose yourself.
You stop chasing validation, you validate yourself.
You stop asking for permission, you give it to yourself.

That is what liberation looks like. And yes, some days will be harder than others. There will be days when self-acceptance feels out of reach. On those days, be gentle. Speak kindly to yourself. Remind yourself that loving yourself is a process, not a destination.

You are not a problem to solve. You are a person to love. So breathe, let go of the pressure. Unclench your jaw. Drop your shoulders and just be. You are allowed to take up space. To rest in your own presence. To be proud of how far you have come.

You deserve a life where you do not have to constantly question your value. That kind of life begins the moment you look in the mirror and say, *"I accept you. I have got you. I am with you."* And trust me that kind of relationship with yourself is a game-changer.

12. CONFIDENCE: THE ULTIMATE ACCESSORY

"Confidence is not about being flawless, it is about being fearless."

No outfit shines brighter than a woman who knows her worth. You have probably seen it before. Someone walks into a room not necessarily the tallest, the loudest, or the best-dressed but you notice them. There is something about them, a presence, a quiet knowing. You cannot look away.

That is confidence. Not arrogance, not attention-seeking, just assurance. A calm, unwavering sense of *self*. And here is the thing: confidence is not about looking perfect. It is not about meeting every beauty standard. Confidence is not even about being the most polished person in the room. It is about being comfortable in your skin, showing up fully as yourself, and not apologizing for it.

That kind of confidence? It is magnetic. It is powerful. It makes people lean in—not because you are trying to impress them, but because your energy says, *"I know who I am."* If you have ever struggled with confidence, you are not alone. So many of us were taught to shrink, to stay quiet, to make ourselves smaller in order to fit. We were told not to be "too much, too loud, too ambitious, too bold", but can I tell you something. You were never *too much*. You were *just enough* for the life you were created to live.

True confidence begins when you stop performing for approval and start embracing who you are even the parts you once tried to hide. It grows every time you show up anyway, even when you are nervous. It builds when you speak your truth, even when your voice shakes.

Confidence is not about never having doubts. It is about moving forward in spite of them. You build it by keeping promises to yourself. By showing up when it would be easier to hide. By walking into that meeting, that date, that dream, not because you are fearless but because you are tired of letting fear lead.

Confidence does not come from having the perfect body, the perfect skin, or the perfect wardrobe. It comes from knowing your value, with or without makeup, titles, or applause. It is the way you carry yourself when no one is cheering. It is the way you speak your truth even when it is unpopular. It is the way you walk into the room like you belong, because you do.

Want to wear the best accessory you will ever own? Start investing in your self-belief. Stop putting off your power until you "feel ready." Ready is a feeling that grows *after* you act, not before. The most stunning women I know are not the ones who meet society's checklist of beauty. They are the ones who own their space. Who walk in purpose. Who lift others instead of competing. Who are honest about who they are and radiate strength from within.

And let me tell you: that kind of confidence? It is irresistible. When you carry yourself with confidence, you send a message *not just to the world, but to yourself.* You remind yourself that you are allowed to take up space. That your voice matters and that you do not need to shrink or edit or hide.

So wear your scars. Let your voice tremble, laugh loudly, walk tall and smile from the inside. Not because you are flawless but because you finally believe you are *enough*. That is the real glow-up. And no designer handbag or trending lip shade can compete with that. You do not need to become someone else to be confident. You just need to become *more of yourself*. And that? That is always in style.

The Myth of Perfection

Self-acceptance does not mean loving yourself *only* on the good days. It means embracing yourself, flaws and all. We are taught that perfection is the goal. That if we just looked a certain way, achieved a certain level of success, or had the "right" personality, we would finally be happy. But perfection is a myth a moving target that keeps us running in circles.

True confidence does not come from being flawless. It comes from owning your imperfections and realizing they do not make you any less worthy. Scars, stretch marks, wrinkles these are not flaws. They are the stories your body carries, proof that you have lived. Mistakes, failures, lessons learned, they do not define you. They shape you. You do not have to be perfect to be influential. You just have to be real.

The Freedom of Saying 'I Am Enough'

Imagine waking up one day and deciding without hesitation that you are enough. Not because you changed, lost weight, gained success, or became what someone else expected. But simply because you *are*.

Imagine no longer measuring your worth by the scale, the mirror, or the approval of others. Imagine fully stepping into who you are, without apology or explanation. That is what self-acceptance feels like. It is not arrogance. It is not complacency. It is liberation. It is the moment you stop asking, "Am I good enough?" and start declaring, "I *am* enough."

Self-acceptance is not a destination, it is a choice you make daily. It is waking up and deciding that you are enough, just as you are. It is choosing to show up, speak up, and live boldly without waiting for permission.

And when you finally embrace the liberation of self-acceptance, you do not just set yourself free you inspire others to do the same. *Confidence is not about perfection, it is about presence. Show up as you are, and the world will adjust.*

13. AUTHENTICITY IS MAGNETIC

"There is an undeniable magic in authenticity it pulls the right people and opportunities into your path."

*W*hat if the very thing you have been trying so hard to hide is *actually, the thing that will set you free?* From the moment we take our first breath, the world starts handing us scripts. We learn early on how to blend in, how to soften our edges, how to fit into neatly labelled boxes so we can be more "acceptable." We are told to speak a certain way, dress a certain way, laugh at the right pitch and dream within limits someone else drew. But what if the real key to joy has nothing to do with blending in and everything to do with boldly being who you are?

There is an undeniable magic in authenticity. It is the kind of quiet force that does not need to shout to be heard. It simply *is* and in being so real, it draws the right people, the right moments, the right opportunities right to your doorstep. Because the truth is, the world does not need another polished replica. It needs you, as you are - fully.

I have seen it happen in ways both small and profound. I think about the people who have left the deepest marks on my heart the ones who were not trying to impress or play a part. They were simply themselves. Honest, unpolished, sometimes messy, always real. And that is what made them unforgettable. That is what made me trust them, love them, learn from them.

Authenticity is magnetic. When you show up as your true self the; you that laughs loudly without apology, that asks hard questions when something does not sit right, that holds firm to your values even when it is unpopular, you start to change the air around you. Some people will be uncomfortable. That is okay, others will breathe easier just by being in your presence, because your courage gives them permission to drop their own masks.

I will be honest being authentic is not always easy. It means risking being misunderstood. It means standing in rooms where not everyone gets you and being okay with that. I have met people who found my strong will or my refusal to simply "go along" a little too much for their comfort. For a moment, it made me wonder if I should tone it down. Be smaller. Less... me.

But time has taught me something beautiful: the very things that unsettle some people are the same things that draw the right people closer. There are souls who *love* that you speak up. Who value that you question instead of blindly agree. Who find safety and joy in the way you show up, honest and unfiltered.

It is a daily choice to keep choosing your truth over comfort. To keep believing that being yourself is more than enough. Because it is. And when you do, you will find you are no longer chasing relationships or opportunities that require you to wear a disguise. Instead, you will start attracting the kinds of connections that see you, really see you and love you not despite your authenticity, but because of it.

There is something rare and irresistible about a person who stops hiding. When you drop the act and let the real you step forward, you do not just free yourself you become a spark that gives others the courage to do the same. And that is where the magic lives. Right there, in the quiet power of simply being you.

14. EMBRACING THE UNSEEN

"The most beautiful parts of you cannot be seen, they are felt".

T rue beauty touches hearts, not just eyes. We live in a world that praises the visible. Glossy images, curated feeds, filtered faces and yet, some of the most unforgettable beauty lies in the things no one sees.

The way you show up for people.
The way you laugh from your belly.
The way you rise again after being broken.
That kind of beauty? It is quiet, but it echoes.

Embracing the unseen is about honoring the qualities that do not always get celebrated: authenticity, kindness, resilience, empathy, integrity. These are not traits that can be captured in a selfie, but they radiate from your spirit, from the energy you carry into every room.

You have probably felt it before that feeling when you meet someone and you cannot quite put your finger on it, but something about them is captivating. It is not their outfit, it is not their face. It is their energy, their light and their sincerity. That is the kind of beauty that lingers, the kind people remember.

When you focus only on the outer, it is easy to feel like you will never measure up. But when you start tending to what is within the way you think, the way you treat others, the way you honor yourself, you begin to glow in a way no filter can replicate. And here is the truth: looks fade, trends change, and what the world calls "beautiful" today may not be tomorrow, but your inner beauty? That never goes out of style. It only deepens with time.

You do not have to look a certain way to be impactful. You just have to be real. Be sincere. Be someone who walks with heart. The world is full of people trying to *look* beautiful. What it needs more of is people who *live* beautifully. Do not underestimate the way your gentleness makes someone feel safe. Or the way your compassion reminds someone that they matter. Or the way your joy lights up a room. Those things? They are priceless.

When you begin to see yourself beyond your surface, when you start to recognize the unseen beauty in your soul, you become unshakable. Because no one can take that from you. It does not fade. It does not wrinkle. It does not need approval. It just *is*.
You are more than your features.
You are more than your body.
You are more than the image the world expects you to fit into.
You are the love you give, the truth you live, the light you carry.

So do not get caught chasing beauty you can lose. Build the kind that stays. Because when you embrace the unseen, you unlock a kind of freedom most people spend their lives chasing. And suddenly, you are not striving anymore you are glowing from the inside out. And the world: it sees that glow, it feels it and it is drawn to it. True beauty reveals itself not in the seen, but in the felt: in laughter, kindness, courage, and love. That is the kind of beauty that leaves an eternal impression.

15. CULTURAL PERSPECTIVES: BEAUTY ACROSS BORDERS

Beauty transcends borders, it is a mosaic of heritage, spirit, and pride."

From Tokyo to Timbuktu, every culture has its own story of beauty. What if beauty was not about fitting in but about standing proud in your uniqueness? Around the world, beauty is seen through different eyes. It is painted in many colors, worn in different shapes, expressed through dance, hair, skin, rituals, and generations of cultural pride. And in each culture, beauty carries stories of resilience, of history, of belonging.

When we only look through one lens, we miss the fullness of what beauty truly is. But when we expand our view, we discover that beauty is as diverse as the world itself. Let us journey across borders and celebrate how different cultures define and honor what it means to be beautiful.

Africa: Lighter Skin, Fuller Bodies, and Bold Features

Across many African countries, beauty is often linked to **full, curvy bodies with rounded hips and thighs**, seen as symbols of health, beauty and womanhood. In countless communities, a woman's curves are celebrated in songs, dances, and local fashion designed to accentuate the waist and hips.

Yet, a more complex narrative runs alongside this. In places like Nigeria, Ghana, Zimbabwe, and South Africa, lighter skin is sometimes still regarded as more beautiful a legacy of colonial hangovers and global media influence. This has led to a widespread skin-lightening industry, with many seeking to achieve a fairer complexion, believing it brings more acceptance or opportunities. It is a stark example of how beauty can sometimes be both a source of pride and pressure.

Middle East: Striking Eyes, Lush Hair, and Full Lips

In the Middle East, beauty traditions often revolve around **dramatic eyes framed by long lashes**, thick, well-shaped eyebrows, and luxurious, flowing hair. With much of the body modestly covered by cultural or religious dress, the face becomes the centrepiece of beauty especially the eyes, adorned with kohl, eyeliner, and eyeshadows that create a gaze both mysterious and captivating.

But equally admired are **full, well-defined lips**, prompting many women to undergo cosmetic enhancements to achieve a plumper look. In places like the Gulf, lip fillers have become almost as common as mascara, reflecting how this particular feature is tied to sensuality and youthful allure. Smooth, glowing skin rounds out the ideal, maintained through time-honored rituals with rosewater, argan oils, and hammam spa traditions that keep beauty deeply linked to heritage.

Europe: Sophistication, Symmetry, and ever-evolving trends

Europe's standards of beauty are as varied as its many cultures, but certain threads run through. Historically, lighter skin, high cheekbones, and delicate features have been idealized across much of Western and Eastern Europe, tied to aristocratic roots and the idea of an indoor, privileged life.

In places like France and Italy, beauty leans into **effortless sophistication** the chic, just-rolled-out-of-bed look that still somehow stuns. In Eastern Europe, you might see more emphasis on statuesque figures, symmetrical faces, and youthful, smooth skin. Across the continent, cosmetic treatments and products promising to preserve youth and symmetry fill countless bathroom cabinets, reminding us how these ideals subtly steer people's choices.

Japan: Grace in Pale Skin and Delicate Features

In Japan, beauty has long been tied to **pale, porcelain skin**, seen as a marker of refinement and elegance. Historically, it suggested a life of privilege, away from outdoor labour. Even today, many women shield themselves with umbrellas and wear SPF religiously to maintain fair skin.

Delicate, small facial features are favoured, with understated makeup that enhances rather than masks. Here, subtlety is the essence of beauty a quiet statement of grace.

India: Lustrous Hair and Radiant Skin

Across India, **long, thick, glossy hair** is almost sacred. Generations pass down hair rituals with coconut and amla oils, while elaborate braids decorated with flowers turn hair into a living jewel.

A glowing, sun-kissed complexion is also celebrated, with turmeric, sandalwood, and saffron used in masks and ceremonies to achieve radiant skin. Jewellery, vibrant saris, and intricate mehndi (henna) designs elevate beauty into a full cultural experience.

Mauritania: Fullness as a Symbol of Wealth and Beauty

In Mauritania, a country in West Africa, beauty standards paint a strikingly different picture from the thin ideals celebrated in much of the Western world. Here, fuller bodies are traditionally seen as the epitome of attractiveness, wealth, and social standing. For generations, Mauritanian families believed that a woman's larger size was a sign that her family was prosperous enough to provide abundantly, and that she herself was prepared for marriage and motherhood.

This deep-rooted ideal led to the controversial practice known as **"gavage,"** where young girls were force-fed large quantities of food and milk to gain weight rapidly. In more recent times, with increasing urbanization and influence from global health narratives, traditional gavage has declined, but it has been replaced in some communities by the alarming rise of hormone or steroid injections to achieve rapid weight gain. These substances, often intended for livestock, are used by some women striving to meet cultural expectations of size even at great personal health risk.

This is a powerful example of how beauty standards, tied to culture and history, can dramatically shape choices about the body sometimes to dangerous extremes. It also highlights how diverse and complex beauty ideals truly are across our world. What is prized in one place may be questioned in another, reminding us that beauty is never a single story.

Iran: The Perfect Nose as a Badge of Beauty

Iran is often called the nose job capital of the world. A **straight, finely sculpted nose** is so admired that many proudly wear their post-surgery bandages as a public sign of beauty investment. It reflects how, in some cultures, altering physical traits becomes a powerful ritual tied to identity and esteem.

China: Fair Skin, Delicate Faces, and Wide Eyes

In China, beauty is a dance of **fair skin, delicate small faces, and large eyes.** Many avoid the sun and use whitening products, linking lighter skin to status. Cosmetic surgeries like double eyelid procedures are common, reflecting a desire for eyes seen as bigger and more open. The "V-shaped" face, with a slender jawline tapering to a delicate chin, remains an enduring symbol of attractiveness.

Brazil: Sun-Kissed Glow and Celebrated Curves

In Brazil, beauty shines under the sun. A **bronzed, healthy tan** paired with shapely curves is the national ideal. Beaches become stages where bodies are celebrated openly, from Rio's Copacabana to Bahia's coast. Confidence whether you are flaunting a tiny bikini or dancing at Carnival is the most attractive feature of all.

South Korea: Youthful Perfection and Flawless Skin

South Korea's multi-step skincare routines are legendary, all aimed at achieving **"glass skin" luminous, poreless, and impossibly smooth**. A youthful, almost doll-like face, big bright eyes, and a delicate jawline drive not just cosmetic trends but entire industries. Here, beauty is meticulous, polished, and often chased through innovative treatments and products.

Beauty Is Everywhere

Is it not striking that what one culture cherishes, another might completely overlook or even avoid. Across all these lands, people wrestle with insecurities about their appearances, proving that the longing to feel beautiful is a truly universal heartbeat.

Perhaps the richest form of beauty is not trying to mirror every standard, but honoring our own, embracing the unique shapes, colors, and stories that make us who we are. Because beauty, in its most authentic form, is not about conformity. It is about standing proudly in the skin we are in.

When you explore how different cultures define beauty, you realize one powerful truth: there is no one right way to be beautiful. Beauty shifts across borders, across generations, and across perspectives.

It is in the Maasai woman with beaded jewellery that tells her story.
It is in the black girl who finally sees her natural hair as her crown.
It is in *you* exactly as you are.

We do not need to erase our differences to feel beautiful. We need to celebrate them. Because together, our differences make beauty richer, deeper, more meaningful. And when we learn from each other, we do not just expand our idea of beauty, we expand our understanding of humanity.

Beauty is not owned by one culture, one color, or one kind of body. It lives in the many, the different, and the deeply personal. Embrace yours, Honor others and let every version of beauty be seen.

16. LETTING GO OF PERFECTIONISM

"The pursuit of flawless robs you of joy: embrace the cracks, that is where your light shines through."

Perfection is a myth that has kept us all from loving ourselves freely. You have been told to aim high, to get it right, to do it perfectly (*which is not bad*). From the way you look, to the way you speak, to how you show up in the world. There is this constant pressure to *be more, do more*, and *mess up less*. And without realizing it, perfectionism becomes the quiet thief of your joy.

I recall a powerful statement shared by a leader I greatly respect that I will always remember: "Make as many mistakes as possible, it is okay. What is not right is repeating the same mistake twice." And true to his word, whenever I or anyone else made mistakes, he never would hold it against us or constantly remind us about it. Through this, he taught me something priceless that it is okay not to be perfect. Society drills into us that there is no room for errors but hearing this was deeply reassuring. It reminded me that making mistakes does not make you a bad person, it simply makes you human. Because we all slip up, we all stumble and that is not a flaw it is life.

Let us be honest, who said you have to be perfect to be worthy? Perfectionism hides behind pretty masks. It says, *"I am just trying to be my best."* But what it really means is, *"I am afraid that being myself is not enough."* And that? That is a lie we have carried for too long. You were never meant to be flawless. You were meant to be real, alive, honest, messy, human and beautiful *because* of it.

Perfection is exhausting. It is the reason you hesitate to show up. The reason you edit your photos, second-guess your words, and replay conversations in your mind long after they are over. It is what tells you not to wear the outfit you love because your body does not "look right" in it. It is what whispers, *"Do not post that. Do not speak up. Do not stand out."* And yet, you keep chasing it, this unattainable version of yourself that only lives in your imagination.

Here is the truth: no one connects with perfection. We connect through truth, through vulnerability, through *realness.* The moment you let people see the parts of you that are still healing, the parts that are growing, the parts that still feel unsure is the moment you give yourself permission to breathe.

There is so much beauty in being undone.
So much strength in the cracks.
So much power in imperfection.

Because imperfection means *you are living.* You are trying. You are risking. You are evolving. And those who truly love you, they do not need you to be perfect. They need you to be *present.* They need your truth, your heart, your essence, not some polished version of you that does not even exist. So let go! Let go of the pressure to always get it right. Let go of the fear of not being enough. Let go of the belief that you have to earn love through flawless performance. You do not.

You are allowed to make mistakes.
You are allowed to be learning.
You are allowed to be a beautiful work in progress.

When you release perfectionism, you make space for freedom, for peace, for creativity and for connection. You stop walking on eggshells and start walking in confidence not because everything is perfect, but because *you are okay with being perfectly human.* That is what makes you relatable. That is what makes you magnetic. That is what makes you *real.* So breathe, unclench your jaw, loosen your shoulders. Let go of the rules you did not write and remember, perfection is not the goal, *presence* is.

You do not need to be flawless to be fabulous.
You do not need to have it all figured out to be powerful.
You just need to keep showing up as *you.*

Because the imperfect version of you, s/he is already enough.

Your beauty does not lie in being perfect: it lives in your truth, your courage, and your willingness to show up anyway.

17. BEAUTY WITHOUT FILTERS

"Raw, unfiltered beauty is the most magnetic kind."

When you remove the filter, what is left is something real and that is rare. We live in a filtered world. We swipe, scroll, and double tap our way through highlight reels that are polished, perfected, and painfully curated. Skin is smoothed, bodies are reshaped, smiles are widened. The lighting is just right, the caption is well-crafted and somewhere in the process... the truth gets lost.

It is easy to forget that behind every flawless photo is a real person. And that behind every filter is someone who, deep down, wondered if their natural self was enough. But what if you stopped hiding behind the filter? What if you chose to be seen in your rawest form, messy hair, bare face, unpolished emotion and said, *"This is me, and I am still worthy"*? That is real beauty.

A story is told of a young woman who would always put on heavy makeup and flawless wigs whenever she went to meet her boyfriend. Layer by layer, she crafted an image she thought he would love. But on the night after their wedding, when she finally washed her face and removed her wig, the man was stunned he barely recognized the woman he had married. What he saw was someone entirely different from the carefully curated version she had always presented. From that day on, he resented her, unable to reconcile the illusion with reality.

As much as we all enjoy enhancing our beauty, there is a quiet power in sometimes showing up without the layers without the heavy makeup, without the mask. Just our honest, unfiltered selves. Makeup is beautiful but let it be light enough to reveal who you truly are, unless you are dressing up for an occasion that calls for a bit of extra sparkle. Because when you strip away the filters, what is left is something rare: something real. And that is increasingly uncommon in our polished, airbrushed world. We scroll through feeds full of highlight reels skin smoothed, bodies reshaped, smiles widened. The lighting is perfect, the captions poetic, but somewhere along the way, the truth gets lost.

It is easy to forget that behind every flawless photo is a real person. Behind every filter is someone who, deep down, wonders if their natural self is enough. Again, there is nothing wrong with enjoying makeup or styling yourself up. Expression is powerful, but the problem starts when we begin to believe that our unfiltered selves are unworthy of love, attention, or affirmation.

You do not need digital edits to be beautiful.
You do not need to angle yourself into someone else's idea of perfection.
You do not need to hide the parts of you that are natural, textured, emotional, or evolving.

In fact, the world is desperate for more *realness*.
We are starving for people who are raw, honest, and not afraid to show up as they truly are.

You have freckles? Show them.
You have stretch marks? Own them.
You have a voice that shakes when you speak your truth? Use it anyway.

When you let go of the filters, both literal and emotional, you give yourself permission to be human. And you give others the permission to do the same. That is where connection lives. That is where confidence is built.
That is where beauty shines brightest.

Think about it: have you ever looked at a photo of yourself and felt disappointed because it did not look like the filtered version? That is the trap. It is teaching us to idolize a false reality. To believe that our beauty must be enhanced to be accepted. You do not need enhancement. You need to remember that the light in your eyes, the texture of your skin, the curves of your body, they are not flaws to be fixed. They are features of a real, radiant, breathing, powerful woman.

The more you show up unfiltered, the freer you become.
Free from the pressure to perform.
Free from the fear of being judged.
Free from the cycle of constantly editing your truth to fit someone else's comfort.

And when you choose to live unfiltered, something powerful happens, people see you. Not the version you think they want but *you*. And those who are meant for you will stay. They will love the laugh lines, the raw moments, the real you.

So next time you catch yourself reaching for the filter, pause.

Ask yourself, *Am I hiding, or am I expressing?*
Am I ashamed, or am I showing up?
And then make the brave choice to show up real even if it is scary. Especially if it is scary.

Because beauty without filters, that is rare, that is bold, that is unforgettable and that is exactly who you are.

You do not always need a filter to be beautiful. Your truth, your texture, your presence just as you are, is already more than enough.

18. THE POWER OF REPRESENTATION

"Representation does not just reflect beauty, it awakens it in those who have never seen themselves."

Representation is not a trend it is a lifeline. It is one of the most powerful tools we have, to redefine beauty. Because when we see someone who looks like us standing in their power, being celebrated, being seen, something inside us wakes up. It tells us, *"Maybe I am worthy, too."*

For so long, beauty was a narrow frame. If you did not fit the mold of lighter skin, straight hair, sharp features, a certain body type you were pushed to the sidelines, told you were *"too much," "too different,"* or just not enough. But the truth is, the mold was the problem not you.

I still remember when l was a young girl the first time I saw someone on the cover of a magazine who looked like me. Her skin was dark, her hair was natural, her smile was radiant. It was not just her features it was the confidence, the unapologetic way she held space. That image did not just say, *"She's beautiful."* It said, *"You are, too."* I did not even know I needed that validation until I felt it. Until I saw what it looked like to be represented, not as an exception, but as a celebration.

That is the power of representation.
It tells the little girl who is been teased for her complexion that

her skin is golden.

It tells the boy with thick, coiled hair that his crown is beautiful.

It tells the woman with stretch marks and curves that her body is art.

It tells the man with scars and softness that his presence is powerful.

The beautiful thing, when one person stands boldly in their truth, they create space for others to do the same. It becomes a ripple; a quiet, unstoppable revolution.

Representation is not just about visuals.

It is about visibility.

It is about seeing people in positions of influence who reflect the fullness of our world.

It is about hearing diverse voices, embracing different stories, and honoring every shade, shape, and story as worthy.

Because when we do not see ourselves in the world, it is easy to believe we do not belong in it.

That is why it matters.

One example that brought me so much joy was the recent announcement from the Miss Côte d'Ivoire 2025 beauty pageant. The organizers declared that they would no longer allow the use of wigs, weaves, or hair extensions during the competition. Instead, contestants are encouraged to wear their natural hair to embrace and showcase their authentic African beauty. This is more than just a rule change. It is a **cultural statement**. It says to every little girl watching: *"You are beautiful exactly as you are. Your natural hair is not something to hide it is something to honor."* That one decision sends a powerful message to our daughters, telling them they do not need to conform to outdated beauty standards to feel worthy, celebrated, or seen.

Representation is healing, it is empowering and it is necessary.

Every ad, every film, every campaign, every boardroom, every book cover, it matters who we put there. Because those faces become mirrors, and those mirrors speak. They say: You are visible. You are valuable. You are beautiful. So, celebrate your features, speak your language, share your story. Because every time you do, you light a path for someone else.

Remember this: you are not too different. You are the difference the world needs. Representation is not about fitting in it is about being seen without needing to change. The more we show up as we are, the more we shift the standard. You are part of that shift. Own it.

19. MEDIA, TECHNOLOGY AND THE TRUTH ABOUT BEAUTY

"In a world of filters, authenticity is your greatest glow."

In a digital world full of edits, choosing to be real is revolutionary. We are the most connected generation in history and yet, we often feel more disconnected from ourselves than ever before. Why? Because we are constantly bombarded with messages about who we should be, how we should look, and what it takes to be *"beautiful."*

From magazine covers to social media timelines, the message is loud and clear: flawlessness is the goal. But here is the truth most people do not say out loud: *that version of beauty is not real.* It is curated, it is edited, it is filtered and it is designed to make you feel "not enough" so you will keep chasing, keep buying, and keep comparing.

You were not born insecure, you were taught to be. You were taught to measure yourself against highlight reels, to believe that your worth was tied to your looks, and to constantly question your value if you did not match the trending look but it does not have to be that way. You do not have to let media define your beauty. You do not have to let algorithms determine your confidence. You do not have to fit into a manufactured mold that was never made with you in mind.

You get to define beauty for yourself. You get to decide what makes you feel radiant. You get to reclaim your reflection from the hands of a society that profits off your insecurity.

Technology can be a beautiful thing it connects us, inspires us, opens up global conversations but we have to be intentional. Because without boundaries, it becomes a mirror that reflects back a distorted version of who we are.

Social media is powerful. It can lift you up or break you down. It can be a tool of empowerment or a weapon of comparison. The key is choosing how you use it and more importantly, how you let it use *you*.

Ask yourself:
- Am I inspired or am I being influenced in ways that hurt me?
- Am I celebrating others or comparing my behind-the-scenes to their highlight reel?
- Am I consuming content that nourishes my soul or content that drains it?

Because the truth is, no number of likes, shares, or comments can validate what you already know deep down: *you are enough*. While technology may highlight appearances, the things that truly matter, the warmth in your voice, the wisdom in your words, the love in your heart can never be captured in pixels.

You do not have to compete with what you see online.
You do not have to wake up every day trying to keep up with an image. You just have to wake up and choose to *be you* present, grounded, real.
Unfollow accounts that make you doubt your beauty.
Mute the noise that makes you shrink.

Follow pages, people, and voices that remind you of your worth not because of how you look, but because of who you are.
When you show up authentically, online and offline, something amazing happens: your confidence becomes contagious. Your story inspires others. Your honesty creates space for someone else to breathe.

That is the real truth about beauty, it is not found in a scroll or a screen.
It is found in moments of truth.
In quiet confidence, in courage and in character.
So take your power back.
Use media and tech to amplify your light not dim it. Show the world that beauty is not an illusion, it is a life lived with authenticity.

You do not need to look perfect for the world. You just need to be real for yourself, because the truest beauty cannot be posted it is lived.

SIMPLY BEAUTIFUL

20. WHEN WE STOP HIDING

"You were not born to shrink; you were born to shine."

Theree comes a moment when hiding becomes heavier than being seen and that is when everything begins to change. We all hide in some way. Behind smiles that do not reach our eyes. Behind hair we straighten or skin we lighten. Behind makeup, clothing, filters, silence. We hide because somewhere along the line, we were told we were not enough.

Too dark.
Too curvy.
Too loud.
Too different.
Too much.

So we learned to shrink, to blend and to fade into the background instead of standing in the light but hiding is exhausting. It chips away at your soul and one day, you wake up and realize you have been spending your life trying to be invisible, just to make others comfortable. Just to avoid judgment, just to fit in and that is when the shift happens. That is when you choose *you*.

I remember the first time I walked into a room without adjusting who I was to match the people in it. My hair natural, my skin glowing, my back straight and my voice firm. I was not trying to impress anyone. I just wanted to be real and in that moment, I felt something I had not felt in a long time, *peace*.

You see, when you stop hiding:
You stop performing.
You stop living under the pressure to be perfect.
You stop needing permission to exist.
You stop apologizing for your presence.
You start owning your space.

It is not easy. Showing up as yourself fully, unapologetically is one of the bravest things you will ever do. It means letting go of masks, letting go of other people's expectations. Letting go of who you thought you had to be just to be loved but let me tell you this: you are worthy of love without the performance.

When you stop hiding, you will lose some things maybe some people, some approval, some comfort but you will gain something far more valuable *yourself*. Once you taste that kind of freedom, you will never want to go back.

You will start to see beauty where you used to see flaws. You will start to speak where you used to stay silent. You will start to walk with purpose where you used to tiptoe. You will stop waiting to be chosen because you have already chosen yourself.

Hiding may feel safe, but it will never bring peace. Real peace comes from alignment. From showing up fully, even when your voice shakes. From being seen and still knowing you are enough. When you stop hiding, you become powerful not because you are perfect, but because you are whole.

The world does not need more polished versions of people. It needs *you*

- ❖ Your rawness
- ❖ Your story
- ❖ Your truth
- ❖ your light.

So wear your natural self with pride. Speak your truth. Take up space. Let people see you, truly see you.

You are not too much.
You are not too different.
You are a breath of fresh air in a world full of masks, and you do not owe anyone the version of you that hides to be accepted.

SIMPLY BEAUTIFUL

21. BEAUTY IN EVERY SHADE

"Every shade tells a story. Every hue holds power."

Your shade is not your shame, it is your story. Your skin is not just a covering it is a statement, a story, and a source of strength. There is something deeply sacred about skin. It holds your history; it connects you to your roots. It is the first thing the world sees but never the full story and yet, for so many of us, our skin has been the reason we have been told we are *"not beautiful enough."*

Too dark.
Too pale.
Too brown.
Too yellow.
Too *different*.

We have grown up with messages that lighter is better, fairer is prettier, and certain shades are more acceptable than others. Those messages are loud. They show up in magazines, in movies, in the workplace, even within our own families. They are lies.

There is no one skin tone that owns beauty.
There is no one complexion that deserves the crown.
There is no hierarchy when it comes to worth.

Your shade is *not* your limitation it is your legacy. The richness of your melanin, the glow of your golden tones, the softness of your ivory skin, it is all beautiful. Not "beautiful for a…" Not "beautiful but…" Just *beautiful.*

When we begin to see beauty in every shade, we begin to heal generations of comparison, shame, and silence. Let us be real colorism is real. In communities across the globe, people have been conditioned to favour lightness. We have seen it in skin-lightening products, in media casting choices, in the way children are complimented.

It hurts.
It scars.
It makes people feel like they need to erase their shade to be seen, but we are rising. We are reclaiming our beauty. We are teaching our sons and daughters to love their dark skin, their brown skin, their glowing skin. We are challenging the systems and stories that told us we had to be lighter to be loved. Most importantly, we are looking in the mirror and saying, "I love what I see."

You do not need to hide from the sun.
You do not need to bleach your birthright.
You do not need to change your pigment to fit into someone else's definition of beauty.

You were handcrafted by something divine. Your skin is not a mistake, it is a masterpiece. And if no one ever told you this before, let me be the one to say it:

Your dark skin is radiant.
Your light skin is luminous.
Your brown skin is powerful.
Your freckles, your undertones, your glow they are all worth

celebrating.

You are not too dark.
You are not too light.
You are *just right.*

Beauty lives in the contrast, in the variety, in the boldness of being different. We need every shade, every tone and every reflection. So, whether you are the colour of deep mahogany, warm caramel, glowing almond, golden peach, porcelain cream, or bronze brilliance you belong. And your beauty matters.

You do not need to change your shade to be seen. Shine exactly as you are because the world is finally learning what you have always known: beauty comes in every color.

22. DARK & DIVINE: A CELEBRATION OF BLACK BEAUTY

"Your skin is not just colour, it is poetry written in melanin, a testament that black is breathtaking too."

Is it not something, how for so long the world tried to tell us what beauty is and what it is not? As if God Himself did not create us in this glorious shade on purpose. As if black was ever a mistake.

Having black skin is a bountiful gift. Truly, are you aware of that? If not, let me help you see it in ways you may never have been told before. Black is distinctive. It is rich, it is complex, it is alive. It carries stories that shimmer beneath the surface.

That extraordinary pigment *melanin* not only gives your skin, your hair, your eyes their magnificent tone, but also serves as your body's natural guardian. It absorbs and scatters the sun's harsh rays, lowering your risk of skin cancer, shielding you from damage that others must buy bottled protection for. It is your armor, woven into every cell by design.

Did you know your melanin even dances with your sleep? It helps produce melatonin, the hormone that regulates your circadian rhythm, guiding your body into rest and repair. That means your beautiful dark skin is not simply decorative it is essential to your well-being. A divine orchestration of biology that speaks to how intentionally you were crafted.

Yet beyond the science, there is a soulful majesty to black skin. It is a story of heritage. To carry blackness is to carry a crown that cannot be removed, no matter how much the world tries to tilt it. Some people will try to diminish this. They will whisper the lie that lighter is better, that you must bleach, cover, tame your natural glory just to belong. But I am here to tell you: black is beautiful too astonishingly, undeniably, heartbreakingly beautiful. You do not need to apologize for your color. You do not need to wash it away or hide it behind layers of someone else's standards.

Own it. Stand in the sun and let your skin glow like polished mahogany and like deep bronze. Smile wide and let the world see that black is not a thing to pity it is a thing to be in awe of. Because your dark skin does not beg for acceptance. It demands celebration. It is not a burden. It is not a flaw. It is your divine signature, written by the same hand that paints sunsets and scatters galaxies.

So do not ever shrink. Do not feel sorry or small or *"less than."* Hold your head high, let your laughter boom, let your beauty radiate from the inside out. Because your blackness is art. It is culture. It is testimony. It is power and that is something the world needs to see more of, not less.

23. BEAUTY IN DIVERSITY

"Beauty isn't uniform. It's countless stories, standing side by side."

Have you ever paused to marvel at a field of flowers? Not one of them is exactly like the other not in shade, size, or shape. And that is precisely what makes it breathtaking. The same is true for humanity.

Look around: people from every corner of the globe carry stories etched into their skin tones, cultures woven into the texture of their hair, legacies alive in the shapes of their eyes and the music of their voices. Beauty is not a single note; it is a chorus. It is only when we try to make it sound the same that the song loses its power.

The overlooked gift of variety

Different climates carved out different features. Heritage painted our skin in hues from ivory to espresso. Geography shaped our bodies, in some places lean from long journeys, in others sturdy from generations of resilience. Even our laughter has different timbres, our dance different rhythms, our traditions their own colours.

And isn't that astonishing? Your features, your very being, carry centuries of adaptation, survival, celebration, and memory. This is diversity. It is not just a nice idea it is a living miracle.

Beyond what meets the eye

Yet beauty in diversity is not limited to how we look. It is also in how we think, dream, create, and connect. The philosophies we hold, the food we eat, the way we raise our children, the songs we teach them all different threads, all part of the same magnificent human quilt.

When you encounter someone whose world is shaped by traditions unlike yours, whose expressions of joy, grief, and hope look different lean in. Ask questions, be curious because true beauty lies in these intersections, where unfamiliar stories open our hearts wider than we ever imagined.

The quiet power of learning from each other

Somewhere, a woman adorns her skin with intricate henna before her wedding, another ties a gele with practiced hands, another steps out with a sleek bob that catches the morning sun. Each one carries dignity. Each one stands in her own lineage of beauty.

When we allow space for different standards, we discover we have much to teach one another. About pride about the freedom to stand as we are, without apology. We realize we can admire another's shine without dimming our own.

A new kind of mirror

Imagine if every time you saw someone different from you, you did not compare or judge, you simply admired. Not in a way that erases the realities of our struggles or pretends biases do not exist, but in a way that genuinely honours the tapestry. Because here's something remarkable: when you see beauty in diversity, you start seeing beauty in yourself, too. The mirror no longer demands

84

uniformity; it becomes a canvas where every stroke adds to the masterpiece. Your freckles, his narrow shoulders, their bold walk. All stunning, all essential.

So maybe it is time we stop trying to fit everything into one idea of beauty. Maybe we let the field bloom wild. Maybe we learn to stand in awe of differences, knowing it is diversity that makes the human family so achingly, gloriously beautiful.

And maybe, just maybe, that's how we finally learn to see ourselves as part of something bigger, brighter, and more breathtaking than we ever knew.

24. STORIES OF STRENGTH: EMBRACING NATURAL BEAUTY

"She embraced herself so fully, so fearlessly, that the world was forced to remember her beauty, forever etched into its memory."

T here is something profoundly powerful about seeing someone stand boldly in their own skin, refusing to shrink or bend to fit a world that once tried to make them feel small. It reminds us that our natural selves are not shortcomings to correct, but stories to honor.

Throughout history, there have been extraordinary women who chose to embrace their authentic beauty women who faced scrutiny and judgment simply for how they looked, yet still rose, undimmed. Their journeys speak to a kind of strength that goes beyond physical appearance; it is the strength of spirit, of self-acceptance, of daring to say, *"I am enough exactly as I am."*

Viola Davis: Unapologetically herself

Think of Viola Davis, a powerhouse in Hollywood known not only for her unmatched talent but also for her willingness to show up raw and real. Viola once shared that early in her career, she struggled to book roles because of the colour of her skin and the texture of her hair. She was told, in so many words, that Black did not sell, that dark did not lead. But she pushed forward anyway with her deep mahogany skin and natural hair that she now often wears proudly on red carpets. When Viola removed her wig on screen in *in one of the movies,* baring her natural hair and her vulnerable self, it was more than just a character moment. It was a declaration to millions watching: *"This is me and this is beautiful."*

Through her courage, she dismantled narrow standards and made space for so many Black women and girls to see their own reflection and feel seen, validated, worthy.

Lupita Nyong'o: A vision of dark, luminous grace

Then there is Lupita Nyong'o, whose very presence has redefined global beauty. When Lupita first burst onto the world stage, winning an Oscar for *12 Years a Slave,* many media outlets seemed surprised to shower praise on a woman whose skin was as richly dark as hers. Because for too long, dark skin had been sidelined considered too much, too "other."

But Lupita did not dim her glow to meet anyone else's comfort. She spoke candidly about praying for lighter skin when she was a child, only to grow up and learn to celebrate the luminous beauty of her own melanin. She stands now draped in vibrant colours, her close-cropped natural hair often adorned with delicate crowns or left completely unstyled a soft halo that says, *"I am majestic exactly as I am."*

Her boldness and grace shattered old paradigms. In her speech at the Essence Black Women in Hollywood event, Lupita spoke words that have since comforted countless hearts: *"I hope that my presence on your screens and in magazines may lead you, young girl, on a similar journey. That you will feel the validation of your external beauty."*

Alek Wek: A dark-skinned revolution in fashion

Then there is Alek Wek, the South Sudanese-born model who walked onto the high-fashion runways in the 1990s a world that had long idolized Eurocentric features and paler skin. When Alek emerged with her deep, stunning ebony complexion, cropped hair, and proud African features, it was revolutionary.

At first, many in the industry resisted. Her look was called "unconventional." Some said she was too dark to be beautiful. But Alek refused to apologize for how she looked.

Instead, she stood taller, smiled wider, and let the radiance of her confidence speak for itself. In doing so, she cracked open the rigid standards of the fashion world. Today, countless young girls with rich, dark skin look at her and see not an exception, but a possibility.

Winnie Harlow: Turning so-called flaws into fierce power

Winnie Harlow, the Canadian fashion model who has vitiligo, a condition that causes patches of skin to lose pigment is another vivid story of resilience. As a child, she was teased relentlessly, called cruel names, and made to feel like her skin made her less.

But instead of hiding or trying to cover up, Winnie embraced her striking difference. She stepped boldly into the spotlight, using her unique look as her signature. Today, she struts down runways and appears on magazine covers all over the world, her contrasting patterns of pigment a living work of art.

Winnie once said, *"I'm not a vitiligo sufferer. I'm not a vitiligo model. I'm Winnie. I'm a model who happens to have vitiligo."* Her story is a powerful reminder that what others may see as flaws can become the very marks that set us apart in the most extraordinary way.

Whoopi Goldberg: Defying every mold

Then there is Whoopi Goldberg, whose very presence in Hollywood rewrote so many unspoken rules. When Whoopi first burst onto screens with her wide, luminous smile, her deep dark skin, her dreadlocks, and her fearless comedic grit, she did not fit the industry's narrow template of beauty or even what leading actresses were *supposed* to look like. And yet, Whoopi never tried to.

She did not straighten her hair or soften her boldness to be more palatable. She did not attempt to wear someone else's version of pretty. Instead, she leaned all the way into who she was her look, her voice, her laugh, her unfiltered, powerful opinions.

Whoopi once shared that when she was growing up, she did not see people who looked like her on TV certainly not people who were celebrated as beautiful or worthy of the spotlight. But by stepping unapologetically into her own skin, she became that person for millions of others.

Today, Whoopi is an EGOT winner (one of the rare few to have won an Emmy, Grammy, Oscar, and Tony) her talent undeniable, her unique beauty unmistakable, her authenticity magnetic.

She proved that you do not have to look like anyone else to be extraordinary. You just have to look like you.

What all these women teach us

Each of these women and many others who 1 have not mentioned chose to embrace what made them different instead of hiding it. They stood in the fullness of who they were, even when the world tried to tell them to change.

They show us that beauty has never lived in sameness. It lives in contrast, in texture, in colour, in stories that break the mold. They remind us that by embracing who we are scars, melanin, curls, unique markings and all we do not just redefine beauty.

We expand it so widely that no one is ever left out again.

25. THE BEAUTY OF GROWTH

"Time does not take beauty away, it adds wisdom to it."

W rinkles do not erase beauty they deepen it. You do not have to stay who you were yesterday, beauty lives in becoming. There is something quietly powerful about growth. It is not always loud. It is not always pretty. It does not always show up as a "glow-up" or a dramatic transformation. Sometimes, growth is invisible. Sometimes, it looks like boundaries. Sometimes, it feels like letting go. But always—*always*—it is beautiful.

We tend to associate beauty with stillness. With capturing the *"perfect"* moment, freezing the best angle, holding on to the version of ourselves we think people love most. But real beauty? It evolves. Just like you.

The woman you were five years ago, she fought battles the world will never know. She did what she needed to survive. And now, you are here. Stronger, wiser, softer in some places and fiercer in others. That is growth and it deserves to be celebrated.

Growth is not about constantly changing yourself to be more likable or desirable. It is about expanding into the fullness of who you are. It is about unlearning what no longer serves you and relearning how to love yourself through every phase of becoming.

It is in the way you now speak up instead of staying silent.
The way you say "no" without guilt.
The way you protect your peace.
The way you show grace to the woman in the mirror instead of criticism.

That is growth.
That is beauty.
And the thing about growth is, it does not always feel beautiful in the moment. Sometimes it looks like crying in the middle of the night because you are finally setting boundaries. Sometimes it feels like walking away from what once felt familiar. Sometimes it is choosing rest instead of hustle, healing instead of performance.

But on the other side of that choice? Freedom.
Freedom to be more of you. And as you grow, you start to realize something: beauty does not live in perfection. It lives in progress, in honesty. and the quiet strength of becoming better, not for anyone else but for *you*.

Give yourself permission to grow without shame, without rushing. And without needing to have it all figured out. You are allowed to evolve. You are allowed to outgrow people, patterns, places and even parts of yourself.

And as you shed old skins, you will uncover new light.
New voice.
New power.
New confidence.

Your beauty does not peak at a certain age or size or stage. It deepens with each experience. Each layer you peel back. Each step you take in the direction of truth.

Let the world see the woman who is not afraid to grow. Who is not afraid to change her mind. Who is not afraid to become softer and stronger at the same time.

You are not behind. You are not late.
You are exactly where you are meant to be growing in grace, growing in depth, growing in beauty.

You are not a finished product, you are a masterpiece in progress. And that journey, in all its layers is what makes you truly beautiful.

26. THE POWER OF PERSONAL DEVELOPMENT

"Grow so deeply within that the mirror becomes the least interesting thing about you."

There is something profound that happens when you start investing in the person you are becoming. Suddenly, the things that used to weigh so heavily the small insecurities, the obsession with physical flaws, the need for surface validation start to lose their grip. Because when you grow what is inside, the outside simply matters less.

Personal development is not about chasing perfection. It is about expanding who you are so your life becomes bigger than what you see in the mirror. It is building a heart that is rich in compassion, a mind that is sharp and open, a spirit that is unshakeable. It is about discovering passions, nurturing talents, and becoming someone you deeply respect so much so, that you stop seeking shallow approval.

I have come to learn that the most captivating people are rarely the ones most outwardly "perfect." They are the ones who have cultivated depth. You see it in the way they listen. In how they show up for others. In the confidence that radiates from knowing who they are beyond titles, beyond trends, beyond physical attributes.

Have you ever met someone whose beauty turned heads whose outward appearance was striking, even captivating but then, the moment they opened their mouth, it all began to fade? You leaned in, hoping for depth, hoping for substance, only to find there was nothing there to hold you.

There is something quietly disappointing about beauty that stops at the surface. No one truly wants to linger long with someone who is shallow, who cannot use their mind to think, to reason, to explore ideas beyond themselves. The most radiant skin grows dull if it is not paired with curiosity, with compassion, with a mind that seeks to grow and understand the world.

Because here is the secret: real allure is layered. It is a mind that sparks with questions. A heart that listens, a soul that reflects, that wrestles, that learns. That is what draws people close and keeps them there long after the first impression fades.

When you dedicate yourself to growing, reading books that challenge you, surrounding yourself with people who inspire you, stretching beyond what is comfortable, you build an inner life so sturdy that superficial concerns cannot shake it.

Suddenly, you are not consumed by the thought of whether your nose is too wide, your hips too full, your skin too dark or too light. You are too busy creating a life that lights you up from the inside. You are too anchored in your purpose to obsess over how others might rank your looks.

Personal development shifts your focus from *"Do they think I am enough?"* to *"Am I becoming the kind of person I want to be?"* And there is incredible freedom in that. Because here is the truth:

Beauty fades.
Skin changes.
Bodies age.

Trends move on.

But a soul that is continually growing keeps seeking wisdom, kindness, and purpose. That kind of beauty only deepens with time.

So pour into yourself.

Learn something new.

Explore places and ideas that expand you.

Heal the wounds that keep you small.

Cultivate joy.

Strengthen your character.

Build a life so rich with meaning that mirrors become little more than a passing glance on your way to something far more important.

When you prioritize who you are over how you appear, something extraordinary happens: your life stops revolving around superficial judgments. You become too full of purpose, too secure in your growth, too busy building something lasting to be weighed-down by shallow standards. That is the kind of beauty no one can take from you because it shines from the inside out.

27. BEAUTY AND WELLNESS: THE HOLISTIC APPROACH

"Real beauty is not skin-deep it is soul-deep, and it thrives where self-care meets self-respect."

W e have been taught to treat beauty like it is something separate. Something you apply, wear, or chase. But the truth is, *beauty is built from within* and your wellness is the foundation.

When your mind is at peace, your glow changes.
When your body feels strong, your posture shifts.
When your heart is nourished, your energy speaks louder than any outfit ever could.

Beauty and wellness are not opposites, they are soulmates. Think about the most radiant people you have met. Were they flawless? No, but they were *whole*. They smiled with their eyes. They moved with grace. They did not just look good, they *felt* good. And that energy? That vitality? That is what makes people unforgettable.

The way you take care of yourself physically, emotionally, spiritually it all shows and no, you do not need an expensive skincare routine or a strict diet to be beautiful. You need gentleness, you need rest. You need movement, joy, hydration, boundaries, laughter and healing. You need permission to put yourself first without guilt.

Because when you treat your body like it is sacred, it responds.
When you treat your mind with kindness, it opens.
When you nurture your spirit, you become magnetic.

This is what a holistic approach to beauty is all about:
Not obsessing over the outer but honoring the whole of you.

- ❖ It is eating food that energize you, not punish you.
- ❖ It is sleeping enough so your body can repair, your mind can reset, your soul can breathe.
- ❖ It is journaling the thoughts that weigh you down and releasing what no longer belongs.
- ❖ It is speaking to yourself the way you would speak to someone you love.
- ❖ It is moving your body because it *can*, not because you hate it.

Your skin will glow differently when your stress is down.
Your eyes will sparkle when your heart is light.
Your presence will shift when your spirit is rooted.

So instead of chasing a look, chase a feeling.
Instead of reaching for a standard, reach for balance.
Instead of trying to be perfect, try being *well*.

Self-care is not selfish.
It is necessary.
It is powerful. It is the soil that allows your beauty to grow without pressure.

You do not have to burn out to be seen.
You do not have to hustle for your worth.
You do not have to neglect your body or silence your needs to be lovable.

You are allowed to be soft.
To be rested.
To be whole.
That is beauty.

Because beauty is not just in the mirror.
It is in your breath.
Your calm.
Your joy.
It is in the way you show up for yourself when no one else is
watching.

And the more you pour into your well-being, the more you
radiate without trying.

The most beautiful glow-up is the one that starts with healing. When you
care for your whole self-mind, body, and soul, you do not just look
different… you become unshakably radiant.

28. YOUR VOICE IS BEAUTIFUL TOO

"Your voice is more than sound; it is an imprint of your soul."

Have you ever paused to truly listen to your own voice? Not just the sound that comes out when you speak, but the essence behind it your opinions, your laughter, your questions, your truths.

Somewhere along the way, many of us were taught to hush our voices. Maybe we were told we were too loud, too opinionated, too emotional. Or maybe we were made to feel that what we had to say simply did not matter. So, we learned to soften our words, to shrink our thoughts, to tuck our stories away where no one could judge them.

But let me tell you something gently, yet with all the conviction I have: **your voice is beautiful too.** It deserves to be heard, not because it is flawless, not because it will always land perfectly, but because it is yours. Because wrapped in every word is your experience, your perspective, your spirit. No one else in this world can speak quite like you do.

I have learned that using your voice does not always mean being the loudest in the room. Sometimes it means asking the hard question when everyone else nods along. It means saying "no" when silence would have been easier. It means telling your story, even if your voice trembles. It means laughing from your belly without worrying who thinks it's too much.

I remember so many moments where I chose to speak up, to seek clarity when something did not make sense, to challenge an idea that felt wrong, to stand by my values even if it made others uncomfortable. Not everyone appreciated it. Some found it intimidating, some even tried to make me feel small for daring to question. For a while, it made me wonder if I should be quieter, easier to accept.

But with time, I realized something profound: the people who matter, the ones who are drawn to truth and light are not threatened by your voice. They are grateful for it. They admire it. They find courage in it to speak their own truths too.

Your voice can be a lifeline for someone else. Your vulnerability, your honesty, your willingness to articulate what many keep buried, that is where real connection begins.

So let your voice be loud if it needs to be. Let it be soft when it wants. Let it question, let it declare, let it wonder, let it celebrate. Let it be uniquely yours. Because beauty is not only found in faces or bodies. It is also found in words that heal, in laughter that fills a room, in ideas that open minds.

Your voice is more than sound, it is an imprint of your soul. Do not tuck it away to please a world that benefits from your silence. Speak up, share your story, and let the world hear your beautiful, irreplaceable voice. Because somewhere, someone is waiting to find the courage to use theirs and they just might find it in yours.

29. THE HEALING POWER OF SELF-LOVE

"Love is the root of healing, and the first place to start is with yourself".

There is a kind of healing that no medicine can offer, no compliment can secure, no external thing can ever truly provide. It is the healing that begins the moment you decide to love yourself not someday, not when you are *"better,"* not when you finally meet someone else's standard but right now, exactly as you are.

Because here is the tender truth:
Self-love is not indulgence.
It is not arrogance.
It is not selfish.
It is survival.
It is the lifeblood of wholeness.
It is the foundation on which everything good in your life will be built.

So many of us have been taught to be hard on ourselves, to measure our worth by what we accomplish, by how we look, by who accepts or rejects us. We have internalized every criticism, every comparison, every subtle message that whispered, *"You are not enough."*

Is it any wonder we walk through life wounded, searching for scraps of validation to soothe the ache? But something changes when you begin to love yourself with the same tenderness you have reserved for others. When you speak to yourself not with condemnation, but compassion. When you stop treating your flaws like enemies and start treating them like tender parts of your human story.

Self-love is not pretending you have no cracks:
It is learning to hold those cracks gently
To pour light into them, to understand that they are what make you beautifully, achingly real.

It heals in ways nothing else can. Because when you love yourself, truly, you stop looking for people or things to prove your worth. You become more anchored. More at peace. More willing to rise from failure, to forgive yourself, to try again. You become less desperate for approval and more confident in your own quiet knowing.

I have seen this firsthand. In my own life, there were days I chased affirmation outside myself like a lifeline. I thought if I looked the right way, succeeded enough, pleased enough, then maybe I did feel whole. But nothing ever filled that empty place until I decided to stop waiting for someone else to tell me I was lovable and chose to tell myself instead.

I started treating myself like someone worthy of care. I learned to rest when I was tired, to feed my mind and body well, to hold my mistakes with grace, to say no without guilt. Slowly, the wounds I carried began to close. Slowly, I began to believe that I was enough. Slowly, peace replaced striving.

That is the kind of healing self-love offers. It does not mean you will never feel insecure or sad or messy again. It just means you have a safe place to return to: yourself. And that makes all the difference.

Self-love is not a final destination you arrive at one day, it is a gentle, courageous practice you return to repeatedly. It is the softest revolution, the quietest miracle, the most profound kind of healing. Give yourself that gift. Because once you do, everything else, every relationship, every dream, every chapter of your life will grow from richer, stronger soil.

30. BECOMING SIMPLY BEAUTIFUL: IN CONCLUSION

"Real beauty doesn't shout. It whispers through your confidence, shines in your kindness, and lingers in the way you live your truth."

You do not need to become someone else to be beautiful you just need to come back home to yourself. For too long, we have been taught that beauty is something you must chase. Something outside of you a standard to reach, a look to perfect, a checklist to complete. The world tells you to pile on more: more products, more procedures, more edits, more ways to hide the very things that make you... *you.*

But what if beauty was never about adding more?
What if it is about peeling back everything that was never yours in the first place?
What if the most radiant version of you is not created it is uncovered?

Letting Go of the Noise

From the moment we are little, we learn how to play roles. We learn to quiet our laughter, to dim our opinions, to mold ourselves into a version that feels safer, more *"acceptable."* We learn to wear masks - polished, careful and curated. And for a while, we may even believe that is what makes us worthy. But each time you hide a part of yourself, you bury a spark of your own light.

Becoming simply beautiful is about letting go of that mask.
It is about releasing the pressure to perform, to perfect and to prove.
It is about choosing to live your beauty and not perform it.

Why Simplicity is So Powerful

Think back: who are the people who have truly moved you in life? Chances are, it was not their flawless skin or symmetrical features.

It was their energy.
Their generosity.
Their unwavering presence.

True beauty is not loud. It is not found in layers. It is felt. It is the warmth that fills a room when someone enters with open-hearted confidence. It is the way kindness softens a face more beautifully than any cosmetic ever could.

Simplicity here does not mean plain or small.
It means real.
It means rooted.
It means knowing that you do not have to do anything extra to be enough.

Shedding What Was Never Yours

Over time, we have all absorbed quiet lies:

- That your nose needs to be sharper.

- That your skin needs to be lighter.
- That your waist needs to be smaller.
- That your hair needs to be straighter.

Ask yourself:
Who told you those things?
Who convinced you that your natural self was lacking?
And more importantly, why did you believe them?
It is time to unlearn those scripts.
Because beauty was never meant to be uniform.
Your beauty was never meant to fit inside someone else's
narrow frame.

I have heard countless stories of women who, after carrying the
incredible weight of pregnancy and bringing life into this world,
find themselves burdened by another weight careless words.
"You are too big now." "You have let yourself go." Sometimes it comes
from strangers, but heartbreakingly, often it comes from the very
partners who once called them beautiful.

A woman's body endures so much. Pregnancy, childbirth,
breastfeeding, hormonal shifts, sleepless nights, stress all of it can
change her shape and size. Even beyond motherhood, life itself
leaves its marks: health challenges, aging, metabolism changes.
Yet so many feel pressured to erase every sign of these seasons,
to wage war against their own bodies just to fit someone else's
narrow ideal.

Some women chase diet after diet, exhaust themselves in the gym
or live in quiet torment, all to shrink back into a version of
themselves that makes someone else comfortable. And when
they cannot, they feel like failures. Their self-esteem fractures.
Anxiety and depression creep in. They lose sight of the woman

who once laughed freely, loved her reflection, and moved through the world with ease.

But here is the truth: it is one thing to care for your body out of love, to nurture it with good food and movement because it deserves health. It is something entirely different to punish it, starve it or hate it into submission.

Your worth does not hinge on a number on a scale or the circumference of your waist. Your beauty was never conditional on fitting someone else's fantasy. The body that may now be softer or rounder than before? It is the same body that carried children, fought battles, healed from wounds, survived every single day with you. It deserves your gentleness, not your shame.

So yes, move your body, feed it well and honor it with care. But never let anyone, not even the one who shares your home, make you believe you must become smaller just to be loved. Because real love does not demand you shrink. It asks only that you be fully, beautifully yourself.

Becoming Simply Beautiful in Practice

This is not just lofty poetry. It is a daily choice. Here is how you can begin to live it:

1. **Choose softness in a world that demands hardness.**
   You do not have to armor up to be powerful. Gentle strength is still strength.
2. **See your flaws through kinder eyes.**
   Your scars, stretch marks, laugh lines, they are not blemishes. They are stories. Proof you have lived.
3. **Stop shrinking.**
   Take up space. Let your voice ring out. Wear the bold colour, say what you mean and stand tall in your truth.

4. **Be curious, keep growing.**
   A shallow mind dulls even the prettiest face. Nurture
   your thoughts, your interests, your soul. Let your
   intellect and empathy be part of your glow.
5. **Treat your reflection like someone you love.**
   Look in the mirror without flinching. Smile at her. Say
   thank you for carrying you through life. Because she,
   just as she is, is breathtaking.

Rewriting Your Beauty Story

Real beauty is not measured by how well you fit into society's
fickle trends.
It is measured by how fully you show up as yourself.
It is seen in the woman who laughs from her belly without
apology.
It is heard in the person who speaks up even if their voice
shakes.
It is felt in the ease of someone who does not need to outshine
because they are already radiant just standing there, honest and
unhidden.

The more you honor who you are, the more your life becomes
an invitation for others to do the same.

Your New Reflection

Imagine waking up and not immediately scanning for what to fix.
Imagine choosing an outfit because it makes *you* happy, not
because it hides *"flaws."* Imagine entering a room with your
shoulders back, not hoping to disappear, but fully present.

That is the quiet revolution. That is what it means to become
simply beautiful. It is no longer begging the world to see your

worth. It is seeing it yourself and letting that truth echo in everything you do.

You do not need another product, another trend, another person's approval to be beautiful.
You just need to remember you beneath it all, untouched, unfiltered and undeniably enough.

So, live your life.
Let your laughter ring.
Let your tears flow when they must.
Speak with conviction.
Rest without guilt.
Love without caution.
Because every time you choose your real self over the world's expectations, you become simply, profoundly, beautifully… you.

And that, more than anything else is what makes you shine.

31. A CELEBRATION OF YOU

"You are a work of art. Not because you fit in but because you stand out."

*B*efore you close this book, there is something I need you to *know: you were always enough.* You have come a long way, now it is time to celebrate the masterpiece you are. You have made it through stories, truths, reflections, and truths that were sometimes hard to face. And through it all, you have shown up. Not just as a reader, but as a woman ready to reclaim the beauty that is been inside you all along.

And if no one has told you lately, let me be the one to say it:
You are radiant.
You are worthy.
You are deeply, fully, completely beautiful.
Not because you fit a standard.
Not because you changed yourself.
But because you dared to be *you.*

You see, I did not write this book just to inspire you, I wrote it to remind you. To remind you of what the world sometimes tries to make you forget: that you are a masterpiece. Not because you are perfect, but because you are real.

I know what it is like to grow up questioning your worth. To compare your reflection to someone else's highlight reel. To feel like you had to change your skin, your hair, your shape, your voice just to belong.

I have been there. But I also know the freedom that comes when you stop chasing and start choosing.
Choosing yourself.
Choosing joy.
Choosing peace.
Choosing *truth*.
And the truth is, you have always had everything you needed. Confidence. Strength. Beauty. Brilliance. It is all in you. This journey? It was never about *becoming* someone else. It was about coming home to yourself.
So here is my wish for you:
That you keep rising.
That you keep unlearning what no longer serves you.
That you keep choosing love over fear, softness over shame, truth over perfection.
That you wake up, look in the mirror, and not just see beauty but *believe it*.
Because you are Simply Beautiful.

In the way you love.
In the way you lead.
In the way you live.
And you do not need anyone to confirm it.
You just need to *own it*.
So, walk tall and shine loud.
And never, ever apologize for taking up space.
This is your story now and it is just getting started.

With all my love.
—Mercy

FINAL THOUGHT

"Be the home you have been searching for; authentic,
whole, and true. You were never missing; only waiting
to be remembered."

Y ou do not have to become someone else to be loved,
you only have to come home to yourself. And when
you do, you will discover the truth that changes everything: you
were **Simply Beautiful** all along.

- ❖ **Be authentic.**
- ❖ **Be truthful about how you feel.**
- ❖ **Be honest with yourself, even when it is hard.**

Practical Steps to Embrace Yourself

1. **Stop Apologizing for Who You Are**
   If you find yourself saying "sorry" for being yourself,
   pause and ask why. You have nothing to apologize for
   when you are simply being you.
2. **Surround Yourself with the Right People**
   Spend time with people who celebrate your authenticity,
   not those who try to change you. Your tribe should
   uplift you, not drain you.
3. **Celebrate Your Wins**
   Big or small, every achievement matters. Take time to
   acknowledge what makes you proud of yourself.
4. **Be Honest About What You Love**
   Whether it is your style, your hobbies or your dreams,
   lean into the things that make you happy, even if they
   are not *"trendy"* or *"popular."*

5. **Practice Self-Compassion**

   You are human, which means you will have days where you doubt yourself. On those days, be gentle. Speak to yourself the way you would comfort a friend with kindness, patience, and love. Remember: one hard day does not define you.

6. **Nurture Your Mind and Spirit**

   Read books that inspire you, spend time in prayer or reflection and sit quietly in nature. Feed your soul the same way you nourish your body.

7. **Be Present in Your Own Life**

   Stop waiting for some future version of yourself to feel worthy. Wear the dress now. Take the photo now. Laugh loudly now. This moment imperfect, alive and honest, is all yours.

8. **Trust That Who You Are is Enough**

   You do not need to do more, be more, or change yourself to deserve joy, love, or respect. You already do. The more you stand firmly in who you are, the more you'll draw in the people, opportunities, and experiences that are meant for you.

9. **Invest in Your Growth**

   Keep developing yourself; read, learn, explore, and ask questions. A well-nourished mind and spirit shine brighter than any outward appearance ever could. When you grow on the inside, it transforms how you see yourself and how the world sees you too.